THE BACKGROUND OF TH

THE BACKGROUND OF
THE COMMON LAW

DEREK ROEBUCK

SECOND EDITION

HONG KONG
OXFORD UNIVERSITY PRESS
OXFORD NEW YORK
1990

Oxford University Press

Oxford New York Toronto
Petaling Jaya Singapore Hong Kong Tokyo
Delhi Bombay Calcutta Madras Karachi
Nairobi Dar es Salaam Cape Town
Melbourne Auckland

and associated companies in
Berlin Ibadan

© Oxford University Press 1990

All rights reserved. No part of this publication may be reproduced,
stored in a retrieval system, or transmitted, in any form or by any means,
electronic, mechanical, photocopying, recording, or otherwise,
without the prior permission of Oxford University Press

'Oxford' is a trade mark of Oxford University Press

First published by University of Papua New Guinea Press 1983
Reprinted with a new Preface by Oxford University Press 1988
Second edition 1990

Published in the United States
by Oxford University Press, Inc., New York

British Library Cataloguing in Publication Data
Roebuck, Derek 1935–
The Background of the Common Law. — 2nd ed.
1. England. Law
I. Title
344.2
ISBN 0-19-585165-X

Library of Congress Cataloging-in-Publication Data
Roebuck, Derek.
The background of the common law/Derek Roebuck. — 2nd ed.
p. cm
Includes bibliographical references and index.
ISBN 0-19-585165-X (pbk.)
1. Common law—England—History. I. Title.
KD671.R64 1990
349.42—dc20
[344.2]
90-40958
CIP

Printed in Hong Kong by Calay Printing Company
Published by Oxford University Press, Warwick House, Hong Kong

For Susanna

Preface to the First Edition

HAVING had the pleasant task for more than thirty years in five common law jurisdictions of introducing the law not only to those studying for university degrees in law, arts, and commerce but also to professional students of accountancy, business, social work, and building, and to all kinds of engineers, police, magistrates, and administrators, I am more than ever convinced that everyone who takes up the study of law needs to know how that law has become what it is. Now that many students have an inadequate education in history, whatever their linguistic skills, they find difficulty with the unfamiliar vocabulary, the strangeness of concepts long ago and far away, and the unavoidable intricacies of English legal development, with its fudges and fictions and its adaptation to new needs by paying the most punctilious lip-service to the rules and policies it was surreptitiously undermining.

Before they know any modern law or even its basic technical language, students of the common law have to cope with a system that places special emphasis on the reports of cases, in which judges declare the law that they are applying. In contemporary litigation of any importance it is likely that reference will be made to reports of cases decided a hundred years ago, and occasionally a decision will turn on a report much older than that. There is no way in which a beginner can be shielded from this reality. What the law is now can only be discovered by examining the process of its development. It is true that there is little time in most courses for the study of legal history but it cannot be denied that we see clearly what the law is only by discovering what it has been.

Beginners who, perhaps at the start of an elementary contract course, have tried, with the help of a law dictionary, to understand what equity is, or real property, or trespass, will know that more is needed. This little book tries to provide it simply. It will help them best if they read it twice, the first time to get an overall picture, the second time more leisurely. Sometimes strict accuracy has been sacrificed to make it easier to understand an idea introduced for the first time. Some important topics have been omitted — the history of constitutional and administrative law, the growth of parliament, the limited company. Authorities are absent; in a book as preliminary as this they would be at least a distraction if not an affectation. But each chapter is followed by the more important references and by recommended reading which I hope will be accessible.

It is not easy for one who has been teaching a course for many years to remember the provenance of ideas he has come to treat comfortably as his own. I have read many times two books, the authors of which every student of legal history should join me in praising. The first is the best for the beginner, Dr J.H. Baker's *An Introduction to English Legal History* (Butterworths, 2nd ed., 1979). The second is that fount of insights and Tacitean apophthegms, Professor S.F.C. Milsom's *The Historical Foundations of the Common Law* (Butterworths, 2nd ed., 1981). Together they have provided a handy compilation, *Sources of English Legal History: Private Law to 1750* (Butterworths, 1986). Where I have borrowed from them without appropriate acknowledgement, I sincerely apologize but blame them for writing so memorably.

Many people have helped me, particularly David Allan and Mary Hiscock of Melbourne University and Frank Bates of the University of Newcastle. This book was the first published by the University of Papua New Guinea Press in 1983. In that endeavour Adri Govers, Sheldon Weeks, and Christopher Pearce showed that hard work and a spirit of co-operation can make something out of nothing.

A particular tribute is due to my tutor, Cecil Fifoot, whose memory is a continuing challenge, as much of style as of scholarship. I am glad of the chance to say of him, as he 'said of Holmes, as he said of Maine, that "he had the gift of imparting a ferment which is one of the marks of genius."'

This reprint, too, is dedicated to my wife, Susanna Hoe, who is responsible for any bits that read well.

HONG KONG   DEREK ROEBUCK
JUNE 1988

Preface to the Second Edition

MORE experience of teaching legal history to beginners and comments from them and colleagues have made a new edition worthwhile. Every page has been rewritten and two new chapters added, on the language and literature of the common law.

I wish I knew enough to comply with the suggestion of the kindest reviewer of the first edition, Professor Wesley-Smith, that chapters should be added on the development of Parliament and the Constitution. His friendly but expert interest, however, confirms my resolve to stick to private law and leave the history of public law to him and others whose attainments fit them to write the modern book beginners need.

I thank my secretary, protector, and tutor in word processing, Ms Sheree Leung, for all her help, not only in making this book.

I know one is not supposed to say anything nice about publishers but my editor, who protocol dictates cannot be named, makes an exception necessary.

My wife, Susanna Hoe, to whom this book is dedicated, is my inspiration and talisman against obscure and self-indulgent writing.

HONG KONG
EASTER 1990

DEREK ROEBUCK

Contents

	Preface to the First Edition	vii
	Preface to the Second Edition	ix
1	Prologue	1
2	Communal Societies and Customary Law	5
3	Anglo-Saxon Law	11
4	Law and Order: the Growth of the Criminal Law	19
5	The Feudal System and the Administration of Justice	30
6	The Writ System and the Forms of Action	41
7	Property: its Invention and Protection	51
8	The Rise of Equity and the Court of Chancery	64
9	Succession and Settlements	70
10	Trespasses and Torts	81
11	Contract and Commerce	92
12	Fictions and Jurisdictions	99
13	The Languages of the Common Law	105
14	The Literature of the Common Law	116
	Appendix: A List of Rulers in England	123
	Index and Glossary	129

1. Prologue

THIS book assumes that the reader is trying to understand what law is about and has accepted that it cannot be understood without some knowledge of its history, that trying to study law without history is like planting cut flowers; moreover that the reader is studying the law of one of the countries which have the common law as at least one of the important sources of their modern law. Throughout the world there are countries which have been and remain profoundly affected by the development of the common law. Most of them were at one time colonies of Britain, in one sense or another, and have adopted or had thrust upon them parts, not of British law, for there is no such thing (Scotland having always had a separate legal system) but of English law, which when distinguished from other systems is known as the common law. Rather in the same way as British postage stamps do not bear the name of their country, those who write about English law have usurped the name of common law, even though there are many other legal systems which have their own authentic common laws, in the sense of a state law which grew to replace the local customary laws of former times.

It is therefore not only the student in England who needs to know the history of the common law. Perhaps it is even more important for students in those former colonies where common law concepts and techniques and ways of thinking about law are still dominant. It is not easy to escape them, and it may not even be wise to try, but if those countries are to avoid being subject to the 'laws of someone else's grandfather' and to create their own indigenous law appropriate to their own circumstances and needs, the next generation of those who will have the responsibility for lawmaking must at least understand the common law. Those countries include Australia and New Zealand (whose only source of law is the common law), India and Pakistan, Canada and the West Indies, Papua New Guinea, Fiji and many other newly independent states in the Pacific, most of English-speaking Africa and Sri Lanka (including those countries which have Roman-Dutch law). Of course the United States of America has been independent for a long time and now no longer looks to England for the development of its law.

But it has itself become a legal colonizer, and not only in Micronesia but in such unlikely places as the Philippines and Japan there are clearly discernible traces of common law influences which have been exported from the United States. Hong Kong is still a colony and its legal system is largely English. Soon it will become a part of China but its constitution, the Basic Law, declares that it will preserve the common law for fifty years.

The story of the common law is a good tale but it is not a romance. Many lawyers have tried to convince themselves and others that it has divine attributes. The modern after-dinner speaker who raises his glass to 'Our Lady the Common Law' has many predecessors. There are plenty of reports from at least the fifteenth century — and there was not much clearly recognizable as common law before then — of statements such as: 'The common law is nothing but common reason', 'Our law is founded on the law of God', and even 'The common law has been for all time since the world began.' But the common law can only be understood if it is seen for what it is: not a romantic ideal or a divine gift or the acme of judicial genius or even the legal aspect of the most politically wise and refined race, but an interesting human construct, the creature of times and places, of economic forces and class interests, of battles for power between political factions and trials of wits between lawyers of great skill and inventiveness.

The breaking down of the reactionary forces of customary law by the creation of central authority and national law, the imposition on royal autocracy of the control of parliament, the wresting of power from the landowning nobility by the middle class, the growth of the welfare state out of the struggles between capital and organized labour, the eventual amelioration of the worst social and economic abuses, are achievements not to be derided.

An English idiosyncrasy, lucky for the historian, has recorded the names of the judicial innovators and of judges who withstood them. The system of reporting cases in common law countries allows the names of judges to stand out in a way they cannot in the anonymous reports of the countries of that other great system, the civil law of continental Europe. We therefore honour the great names of Coke and Bacon, the giants of law and equity respectively; of Mansfield, the father of the commercial law who raised both the practical and intellectual standards of the courts; and of course the paragons of the present time. It is true that Coke spoke straight to the tyrant James I, but he then fell on his face and begged forgiveness and he was a lawless bully of political prisoners. Bacon was not only Lord Chancellor, he was the greatest scholar of his time. But he was sacked for taking bribes — from both sides, which does not seem intelligent. Mansfield is always credited with the immortal saying that the air of England is too pure to admit of slavery. It was not he who said it but counsel in *Somerset's Case*, over which Mansfield presided. His own role was less laudable. Though it was a *habeas corpus* action, that is a constitutional demand that someone wrongly detained be set free, Mansfield was more concerned with the economic loss to slaveowners from his doing justice. He adjourned the case twice in the hope that the parties would settle the matter quietly and not cause trouble by creating a precedent whereby even more black slaves in England would have to be released. Throughout the common law world today there are judges still who will, consciously or not, decide the way the government wants them to rather than according to law.

That the law was not created by angels should not surprise any student, and may increase the likelihood of it retaining his or her interest. Whenever the flattering picture is presented of a lawyer bravely, selflessly and skilfully standing up for justice, remember there is one on the other side, too. It is a mistake to confuse law and justice. Law is a system evolved by people in society for the solution of problems thrown up by life which the affected parties cannot resolve for themselves or which society — the group or the State — has decided that the parties ought not to decide for themselves. If society decides that a particular kind of problem is appropriate for its intervention, then it imposes solution-bearing techniques. That is how law resolves conflicts. But law also has a prophylactic function. It must guard against and try to prevent conflicts. To do that it provides standards and sanctions or punishments so that individual people may forecast the result of their behaviour and the behaviour of others. Law sometimes facilitates the affairs of life. It enables you to dispose of property by will, to form a limited company, to adopt a child. Law is one means whereby the group, whether it is a small community in communal society or the State in a more technologically advanced one, tries to impose order on nature. Law is one of the tools which human beings have devised to deal with the social problems of life, in the same way that they have invented machines to help them to control the physical nature around them.

All law is like that, whether it is the common law or French law or Soviet law or customary law of the present day or Anglo-Saxon England. Moreover, other legal systems have gone through stages of development similar to those of the common law. There are startling analogues of English legal moments in continental legal history, even a Magna Carta in Hungary, the Golden Bull of Andrew II (1222), and most legal systems can show a similar shift from communal to State law. Yet the common law has its own unique history and special relevance for students in what are still described as common law countries. The following chapters are attempts to sketch the background of some of the more important parts of that history.

REFERENCES AND FURTHER READING

Sommersett's (or Somerset's) Case (1772) 20 State Trials 1.

2. Communal Societies and Customary Law

COMMUNAL SOCIETY

The word primitive in such phrases as 'primitive law' and 'primitive society' is misleading. 'Uncivilized', in the sense of 'without cities', though technically accurate, has a similar pejorative sound. What is really meant is non-urban, belonging to a stage of human development, found everywhere in the past and still existing in a few places, in which people's lives are ordered in a quite different way, where social and economic relations are common not to a nation but to a small ethnic group. For convenience I call that kind of society 'communal'.

Wherever people are found, at whatever time in history, they are social animals. If circumstances force them to be alone, such as the need to hunt, they seek to rejoin the group when they can. It may well be that a permanent grouping is necessary for the survival of human young. The smallest group, the family, is in communal societies larger than two generations: it is not just a mother, a father and their children. These extended families have relations with other groups and wider kin and they congregate in larger groupings at fixed times or for agreed purposes. Even hunters and foodgatherers, like the aboriginal Tasmanians, who were scattered at the ratio of one to every seven square miles, came together in large congregations for consultation and the performance of ceremonies and for other social reasons.

All these groupings required appropriate rules of conduct. Just as a child in western society learns the rules of living of its own family, then of school and to some extent of the whole group (the important rules of conduct though not, of course, the whole of the law) so a child in a communal society learns the rules of its family and, sometimes through formal initiation, those of the larger group.

Between the largest grouping, the nation, and other nations, there is no law which can be imposed by legal sanctions, for the most part. International law is not like that. That does not mean that international law is unimportant or powerless. It does not mean that it is not really law. It means that there is no superior force which can stop it breaking down, can stop the anarchic alternative: war. So in communal society there is no superior power which can control the breakdown of customary ways of dealing with tribal disputes.

CUSTOMARY LAW

Within the ethnic group, however, there are rules which have greater sanctions than the law has in technologically advanced societies (which I call for convenience 'developed'). Life in a communal society is public. There is little privacy or opportunity for individualism. Eccentricity is less tolerated. There is little chance of antisocial conduct passing unnoticed or being attributed to the wrong person. Moreover, the sanctions are often immediate, intended to fit the crime, and are often applied until they work, that is, until the culprits give up their anti-social behaviour and admit their faults, or have their capacity for such activities removed.

The rules are unwritten, but better known in their entirety than the laws are to citizens of developed societies. The greatest technological advance, so far as the law is concerned, is the use of writing, which reduces individual and communal memory as it provides the techniques of recording and reminding. But the basic difference between communal and developed societies is economic. Economic relations are far more complex in developed societies. A great deal of the complexity of their law is a result. On the other hand, a great deal of the complexity of communal law results from communal society's concern to control much more of what in a developed society would be considered the private life of its members.

Urbanization presupposes mobility of small family groups. With it comes industrialization and eventually capitalism. These increase the complexity of economic laws, but make impossible the policing of rules of private conduct. The relations between a man and his mother-in-law may be controlled in a communal society with refinement, so that he may not speak of her or even allow his shadow to fall on her, and breaches of these rules may incur severe penalties — divorce or even death. Developed societies attempt no such control and its last echoes are heard only in tired jokes. Communal societies have comparatively few members and the selection of spouses is limited. For the health of the group it must be controlled by wider definitions of incest. All the members of a communal society know those rules in detail and expect hard punishment for their breach. There are everywhere in communal societies legal rules of a complexity, sophistication and abundance that lawyers in developed societies find hard to comprehend. On the other hand there are no rules at all to deal with everyday matters of a developed society: banking and insurance, safety at work or on the roads, labour relations or rent restriction.

THE SHIFT FROM KIN RESPONSIBILITY

The progress of law in communal societies is often said to show a shift from the responsibility of the family or kin to individual responsibility. But the change from communal to developed is not away from family responsibility to family towards individual responsibility to individual. Modern law emphasizes instead the responsibility of the individual to the State. Sir Henry Maine is famous most of all for his dictum: 'The movement of the progressive societies has hitherto been a movement from Status to Contract.'

The movement of the progressive societies has been uniform in one respect. Through all its course it has been distinguished by the gradual dissolution of family dependency and the growth of individual obligation in its place. The individual is steadily substituted for the Family, as the unit of which civil laws take account ... Nor is it difficult to see what is the tie between man and man which replaces by degrees those forms of reciprocity in rights and duties which have their origin in the Family. It is Contract. Starting, as from one terminus of history, from a condition of society in which all the relations of Persons are summed up in the relations of Family, we seem to have steadily moved towards a phase of social order in which all these relations arise from the free agreement of individuals.

This impressive and influential statement is not based on any first-hand enquiry into communal society, and cannot be made to fit the understanding we now have. In the nineteenth century, legal scholars and political philosophers believed that contracts took their force from the will of the parties. Now we know better. The will of the parties has no effect unless the State lends its sanctions. Moreover, if there ever was a natural shift from status to contract, it has certainly passed. Less and less, not only in socialist countries, is left to the power of the individual and more is controlled by the relevant group, the State. Consumer sales on credit are governed by legislation protecting the consumer and thereby restricting the freedom of the seller and lender; ownership of land is controlled by planning legislation; hours of work, minimum wages and working conditions are all controlled; and the list grows as the need to provide rules for the new complexities of developed society is increasingly recognized.

As societies become developed, laws are elaborated to fill the needs created by new complexities of social organization and new conflicts of interest. There is a shift away from the responsibility of one kin to another kin. The responsibility of the individual to the larger group, the State, takes its place.

CUSTOMARY LAW AND NATIONAL LAW

Is the difference between developed law and communal law merely then that the economy of the former is on a larger scale? There is enough evidence to show that this is not so, and that there is some qualitative change, but this should not be exaggerated or romanticized.

The pre-scientific attitudes of developed societies are slowly being displaced. We no longer burn witches or compel people to go to church but there are disabilities still which apply to acts done in England on the Sabbath, and we still swear oaths and require our judges to wear exotic costumes. We do not consider it appropriate or necessary to exact vengeance and carry on blood feuds against the tribe of the person who has committed adultery to the shame of the spouse or the group, but in some common law countries damages are still recoverable for stealing a wife. We do not indulge in tribal warfare over boundaries or cattle or insults to the gods or group, but religious leaders demand death for blasphemy and we have not progressed very far in the creation of agencies to enforce peace, and disarmament still has to be worked for. Our folly in allowing ourselves to be governed by those who send nuclear devices spinning round the world should not allow us to feel superior to those we call primitive, who still have enough sense and technological skill not to destroy their environment.

It is clear then that it would be rash to say that law is in all ways more subtle, fairer to the individual, or productive of the well-being of the group in developed than in communal societies. There are, however, some basic differences. The law of developed societies has categories, used for the purposes of exposition and application. Communal law does not, all law being one, consecrated by use, general acceptance, and religion (whatever that might mean in any society). Communal law cannot be questioned on grounds of utility. It is an essential attribute, it belongs to the group in the same way as its religion, of which it is often seen as a part. There is, nevertheless, continual change, but not consciously engineered, to meet changing situations, particularly the need to accommodate a colonial administration. But new law is seen as a development of old law, and legitimately a part of it. Civilisation must be far advanced before the idea of progress emerges and with it conscious law reform.

There are some lessons to be learnt. They are obvious but hard to accept. Human beings have evolved a clever system of rules for ensuring that the group continues and is not destroyed by strife. They have not, however, worked out how to provide a system of sanctions to enforce those rules on warring nations. If two African or Papua New Guinean or Aboriginal tribes went to war in the days of the Empire, there was the superior technology of the colonial administration to put power into the sanctions imposed from above. There is no such world power to stop war. But that is only the more obvious problem. Within and across societies, the economic relations distribute power unequally, so that friction is inevitable. Even if war between nations can be outlawed, war between classes, between the privileged and those whose exploitation is necessary for those privileges, cannot be prevented by any superior force (for there is none conceivable) but only by rules, laws, which prevent the conflict of interest, the split into privileged and poor, among nations as among individuals.

It may be that the only basic difference between the attitudes of developed and communal societies to law is that the former understand that every system of law is in continual need of improvement and that something should be done about it. It may also be that, while people in developed societies manage with luck to cling to existence, communal societies (with the assistance of developed societies) are almost everywhere becoming extinct. There is, of course, the further possibility that developed societies will destroy their own means of life, leaving the human race to survive only in communal groups with the social and ecological skills made necessary by disaster.

REFERENCES AND FURTHER READING

Maine, Sir H., *Ancient Law: its Connection with the Early History of Society and its Relation to Modern Ideas*, Sir F. Pollock ed. (John Murray, 1912). This is the best of many editions.

Mair, L., *An Introduction to Social Anthropology* (Clarendon P., 2nd ed., 1972, especially Chapter 9 'Law').

Roberts, S., *Order and Dispute: An Introduction to Legal Anthropology* (Penguin, 1979).

3. Anglo-Saxon Law

COMMUNAL LAW IN ENGLAND

In about AD 535, Roman law was codified in the *Corpus Juris* which the Emperor Justinian's law reform committee produced. In 597 Christianity was reintroduced into England from Rome. The Roman law was portable but did not flourish in England. Rome was a developed society. It had long since passed its prime and had almost completed its decline. England was still in its infancy, its law and its society still communal. The economy of England at the start of the seventh century was quite incapable of allowing a successful graft of Roman law. From that time until the Norman Conquest in 1066 is the period of the Old English, the Anglo-Saxons, as distinct from the Saxons on the continent of Europe. The legal history of that period is the history of the shift from group-to-group responsibility to individual-to-State responsibility.

It is important not to assume that most things were the same then as now; in particular there were no police, and no justice separate from administration. Justice and administration were the same thing until the end of the Middle Ages in England, as they were until modern times in Japan and are still, to all intents and purposes, in China. There was no central government, but rather large tribal areas belonging to the different 'nations': Angles, Saxons, Jutes. By 800 Wessex was supreme, until Danes invaded and made great inroads into 'English' territory. By 900, Wessex had reconquered; by 1017 Danes were in control of all England. It was a tribal and a bloody life. There was little 'law and order' outside the tribal group. The Celts had huddled in little enclosures. The Anglo-Saxons were invaders, and robber bands have strong leaders. When they settled, they built spacious and populous villages on the manorial system. Their warrior chiefs became their peacetime lords and protectors.

Law was still customary, but the king could declare its details for the education of his people. King Ethelbert I (560–616) in Kent and King Ine (688–726) in Wessex gave laws, making sure that there were payments both to the person wronged and to the Crown. Not only was law undistinguished from administration, it was sold at a price and was a valuable source of revenue to its 'owner'. The village headman was the lord's man, the reeve, who presided over the manorial 'court', which was a general meeting to transact all kinds of business of the manor.

ALTERNATIVES TO THE FEUD

The development of English law was by improvement of administration, in particular by substituting for tribal fighting or blood feud a system of criminal and civil justice, the same for all people of equal rank, administered eventually not by neighbours or families but by impartial outsiders. That was a long time coming. The first step to ending the blood feud — the universal answer of customary law to serious conflict in communal society — can be seen in such steps as set out in the law of King Alfred (871–901):

Law 42. Also we enjoin, that a man who knows his adversary to be residing at home, shall not have recourse to violence before demanding justice of him.
  1. If he has power enough to surround his adversary and besiege him in his house, he shall keep him inside seven days, but he shall keep him unhurt for thirty days, and send formal notice of his position to his kinsmen and friends.
  2. If, however, he flees to a church, the privileges of the church shall be respected, as we have declared above.
  3. If, however, he has not power enough to besiege him in his house, he shall ride to the ealdorman and ask him for help. If he will not help him, he shall ride to the king before having recourse to violence.

By the time of King Athelstan (924–39), the person wronged had to summon the wrongdoer before three successive borough courts. Even if the wrongdoer failed to answer the summons, it was the leading men of the borough, not the plaintiff or his kin, who rode against the defendant and took him and all he owned and put him under surety. In Saxon as in Roman times you were in trouble if you could not get someone to stand surety. The intention was clearly to get the parties to the conflict to settle out of court, and a helpful painkiller and assuager of injured pride, then as now, was delay.

The seventh, eighth and ninth centuries in England were marked by invasion and internal strife. From 850 onwards the rulers were

Norsemen of some kind. In such times it was natural that all should look to their lord for protection and that he should be able to call upon their services in war and peace. He was the rallying point of an army and the protector and seed-giver. In return he took fealty. There were therefore in England before the Norman Conquest some but not all the elements of a feudal system. But royal administration depended on the lord's administration. The lordless man was a matter of administrative concern. The shift is clear from kin responsibility to lord's responsibility but it was not yet individual to State. The lord must stand surety (*borh*) for his man, both for his appearance in court and eventual payment of compensation. If a man had no lord he could be proclaimed an outlaw — outside the law — and he lost his legal rights because he could claim no lord's protection.

COMPENSATION

The concomitant of the shift from kin law was the shift to compensation instead of feud. As early as King Ethelbert in 597 there was a tariff. Special penalties protected the clergy, who, though still a new phenomenon, were a vital part of central authority. The king laid down the rules of his peace, so did the lord, and so did the bishop. The peace was the ambit of the great man's protection. To break it was to question if not to threaten his authority. Therefore a breach of the peace had a twofold penalty, one to the wronged individual and one to the king, or lord, or bishop. There were geographical limitations on the exercise of authority, and administration depended upon the personal qualities and resources of powerful individuals. As usual in communal societies, there was no distinction between civil and criminal matters. All was transacted in the 'folk-moot', the all-purpose assembly, but the sanctions were what would now be considered criminal sanctions and were imposed for failure to sort out the conflict amicably, or rather according to the customary and proper methods.

It was the responsibility of all, not just the parties, to see that the king's peace was kept. King Athelstan (924–939) ordered all bishops, aldermen (earls) and reeves to keep it.

When Canute established a Danish kingdom in England, he imposed fines on those who did not perform their public duty of seeing that the king's peace was kept. The man who found a thief had to raise the hue and cry and join the *posse comitatus*, the group who were bound to chase the thief and bring him to justice. By 1000 the whole community had been put in the place of the kin and were responsible for the individual's behaviour. But this could not be allowed to water down responsibility; therefore, by Canute's laws, every man who wanted the privileges of a free man had to be in a tithing, a group of 10 men, who were each and all automatically bound to stand surety for each of their group. Every male above the age of 12 must belong. Each tithing was in a hundred, a group of 10 tithings, which was a forerunner and did some of the work of a police force or militia.

Wessex was divided into shires, and the kings of Wessex, after Alfred had unified England, imposed the shire system on the rest of England. The nuclei of economic and social activity were the boroughs, many of which were the fortified places of former wars. All boroughs had folk-moots where the king's man presided. In the tenth century the geographic unit, the hundred (or *wapentake* in the Danish part of the country called the Danelaw) became the generally accepted administrative unit, though it certainly had nothing to do with 10 tithings. Perhaps it equalled 100 hides, which were a measure of land not always of the same size. An ordinance of King Edgar in 960 says that the shire court must be held twice a year, the borough court three times a year, and the hundred court every four weeks. Of course these courts were not like modern law courts but were all-purpose administrative meetings.

The characteristics then of that period of development were the transmuting of feud into legal action and the use of what has been called the procedural contract to deal with such things as cattle theft, one of the most difficult and prevalent problems of Anglo-Saxon society.

The first step was to provide substitute remedies and a system to enforce them. The system of wergilds, set amounts of compensation depending on the nature of the injury and the status of the injured, provided the remedies. For example, from the laws of King Ethelbert (601–04):

These are the decrees which King Ethelbert laid down in the days of Augustine.
   1. For God's property and the Church's twelvefold wergild; a bishop's property elevenfold; a priest's property ninefold; a deacon's property

sixfold; a clerk's property threefold; breach of the Church's peace twofold; breach of the peace of an assembly twofold.

2. If the king calls his people to him, and anyone harms them there, he shall pay twofold compensation, and 50 shillings to the king.
3. If the king is feasting at anyone's house, and any sort of offence is committed there, twofold compensation shall be paid.
4. If a freeman robs the king, he shall pay a ninefold wergild.
5. If one man kills another on the king's premises, he shall pay 50 shillings compensation.
6. If a man kills a free man, he shall pay 50 shillings to the king for breach of his seignorial rights.
10. If a man lies with a maiden belonging to the king, he shall pay 50 shillings compensation.
11. If she is a grinding slave, he shall pay 25 shillings compensation. If third class, 12 shillings.
14. If a man lies with a nobleman's serving maid, he shall pay 12 shillings compensation.
16. If a man lies with a commoner's serving maid, he shall pay 6 shillings compensation; with a slave of the second class, 50 pennies; with one of the third class, 30 pennies.

SURETIES AND ENFORCEMENT

But enforcement was not so easy. That is why sureties were important. From the laws of Kings Hlothere and Eadric (685–6):

8. If one man brings a charge against another, and calls him before an assembly or meeting, the latter shall always provide the former with a surety, and render him such satisfaction as the judges of Kent shall prescribe for them.
9. If, however, he refuses to provide a surety, he shall pay 12 shillings to the king, and the matter shall continue open as before.
10. If one man charges another, after the other has provided him with a surety, then three days later they shall attempt to find an arbitrator, unless the accuser prefers a longer delay. Within a week after the suit has been decided by arbitration, the accused shall render justice to the other and satisfy him with money, or with an oath, whichever the accused prefers. If, however, he is not willing to do this, then he shall pay 100 shillings, without giving an oath, on the day after the arbitration.

As examples of how these laws worked, it is interesting to see how the problems of cattle theft (and sales) and wills were dealt with.

SALES

There were elaborate enactments dealing with pursuit, arrest, conviction and punishment of cattle thieves from Ethelbert to Canute. King Wihtred (690–725) and King Ine (688–725) provided harsh penalties for cattle theft: death, slavery for the thief and his family, cutting off a hand or foot. If the thief was caught in the act he could be killed on the spot; if discovered with the cattle still in his possession, there followed the procedural contract — the owner grabbed the beast by one ear, the possessor grabbed the other and each claimed ownership. The possessor provided sureties and the matter went to court. It is at this stage impossible to distinguish the law of theft from that of sale, because the usual defence was that the possessor had bought the cattle in good faith. The possessor might be able to produce the seller from whom he had bought the cattle, who would support his claim to have lawfully bought them but, if the seller could not be found, then it was up to the buyer to produce the witnesses which the law required should attest every lawful sale. When the sale of cattle took place, the parties and witnesses assembled in the market square. The witnesses inspected the beasts for signs of ownership, the seller's brand or earmark, then listened to what the parties said, which would be in a well-known formula. They would then be available in a later dispute to swear to what the parties promised. Absence of such witnesses was convincing evidence that the possessor had not acquired the cattle legally.

WILLS

Even more interesting than sales in some ways is the Anglo-Saxon written will, a technique which was encouraged if not introduced by the Church. Professor Hazeltine described it neatly:

The Anglo-Saxons think in terms of grantor and grantee; and by grant they mean both conveyance and contract. The king and leading laymen form a large part of the class of grantors; while the ecclesiastics and ecclesiastical institutions are one of the largest, perhaps the largest, class of grantees. These grantors and grantees are traffickers. The subject-matter of their bargaining is not, however, spears or chasubles: these two groups of men are concerned with other things of far greater durability and value. The men of this world want things in the next, while the men of the next world want things in this. By their gifts the lay folk buy things in the spiritual world; and by their counter-gifts and counter-performances the clerical buy things in the corporeal world. Rights in terrestrial possessions are exchanged for rights in heavenly mansions; and these rights are exchanged by grants which at the same time are contracts.

Those grants were, like other transactions, carried out by solemn words before the required witnesses. But to make sure that no disappointed family would challenge and upset a grant to the Church to take effect on the death of the grantor, who was no longer there to admit the grant, the priests (who commanded the technology of writing) invented a technical device more permanent than the memories of the mortal witnesses: the written will. In Anglo-Saxon times it remained merely a memorial of a transaction, a grant made orally before witnesses. The grantor granted land to the Church, in the hope that he would be favoured in heaven: 'with great humility we pray that in heaven we may join the company of those who have been lords on earth and of the men who have given their lands to the Church.'

The Church had other techniques to offer the law. Salvation was not only an inducement to grant land to the Church. It could be used as security for the enforcement of contracts. A law of King Alfred of about 890 declares: if A alleges that B has not carried out what B promised to God as surety, A shall support his allegation by an oath sworn in four churches. B may clear himself by swearing to the contrary in 12 churches. Anglo-Saxons not only believed in the effectiveness of divine punishment for swearing a false oath: they believed that their fellows believed in it too. This technique was further elaborated. The promisor might pledge his faith, by depositing as security with some third person, typically the bishop, his chance of salvation, only to be redeemed by the performance of the promise.

ANGLO-SAXON ORIGINS

Arguments continue about the origin of the elements out of which were created the foundations of the common law. It would be a mistake to believe the champions of the 'English', who try to find an Anglo-Saxon origin for all to the exclusion of Norman imports and inventions. Nevertheless it is clear that before the Norman Conquest in 1066 there already existed in England two of the cornerstones of those foundations: the king's peace and the administrative and legal responsibilities of local communities. A third cornerstone, the writ (with its servant the sheriff), was in existence, though at best rough hewn, when the Normans came. The unquarried stone for the fourth cornerstone, the jury, was found, perhaps in the group of men sworn in to make inquiries, though it was fashioned with tools brought from Normandy only. Later chapters will show how important the king's peace, the sheriff, the king's writ and the jury were to be, not only in the spread of effective administration but in the change from customary law prevailing only in its own group to a common law for all the kingdom.

REFERENCES AND FURTHER READING

Attenborough, F.L., *The Laws of the Earliest English Kings* (Cambridge U.P., 1922).

Baker, J.H., *An Introduction to English Legal History* (Butterworths, 2nd ed., 1979, cited hereafter as Baker and referable to all later chapters).

Harding, A., *A Social History of English Law* (Penguin, 1966, hereafter cited as Harding and referable to all later chapters).

Hazetine, H.D., 10 *Columbia L. R.* 617.

Pollock, F. and Maitland, F.W., *The History of English Law* (Cambridge U.P., 2nd ed., 1898).

4. Law and Order: the Growth of the Criminal Law

THE criminal law is the most basic part of any legal system. Preservation of order and control by the group of anti-social behaviour of individuals are the primary needs of society and upon them are based all the protections and opportunities which society offers. The group must do what it can to state emphatically that certain acts are not only wrong but will incur sanctions from the group. Murder, assault and theft are widespread if not universal examples of such acts. The test of a healthy society, however, is not only whether it is orderly and able to control anti-social behaviour: it is also necessary to show that order is not the product of arbitrary repression but of law.

CRIME AND THE CONQUEST

If a central government is to claim that it controls the whole country, it must show that it accepts responsibility for its orderly administration and discharges that responsibility adequately, either directly or indirectly. William the Norman in 1066 was determined to establish that kind of control over his newly conquered English colony. The task which his successors saw as primary for centuries was to elaborate that control and monopolize it. The development was not without its setbacks. There were many times when rebellion was raised, sometimes there was anarchy and once successful revolution.

Later chapters will show how some of the organs of administration developed: courts, judges, procedure. In most countries nowadays it is assumed that procedures for criminal matters will be different from those for civil cases and there may well be different courts. But for a long time after the Norman Conquest, not only were what we should now call civil and criminal matters dealt with by the same procedures in the same courts, but the substantive law of crimes (so far as it is possible to speak of such a thing) was not differentiated from other law.

The last chapter showed how the Saxon kings promulgated laws with tariffs of compensatory payments intended to supplant private retaliation and put the responsibility for law and order on the community. The Norman kings and their successors strove by extending the idea of the king's peace to assume that responsibility themselves. It must be remembered that the jurisdiction to hold a court was thought of as a valuable property, and was owned by great landowners and churchmen, who were not happy to cede such a valuable source of income to the royal government. Even as late as 1846, Sir Oswald Mosley was able to sell his right to hold a Court Leet (the customary court of his manor) to the burgeoning borough of Manchester for £200,000.

Chapter 10 will show how the law of civil wrongs grew out of the undifferentiated law. This chapter is concerned with the separation from that bulk of what became the criminal law. The distinction between public wrongs (or crimes) and private wrongs (or torts) is easy to describe. The former are the concern of the State. They are punished by the State as threats to the peace and orderly government of the whole community. The latter are the concern of the individuals affected, who may seek compensatory redress for the injuries they suffer from those who have harmed them — or may, if they prefer, do nothing. Yet the early law makes no such sharp distinction. The laws of King Ine (688–725) or Alfred (871–901) look from one aspect like lists of compensatory payments. From another they were the most sophisticated machinery then available for protecting the community from the threat of self-help or tribal fighting. One aspect shows the king's central government legislating and involving itself in all manner of otherwise private disputes, exacting money payments for itself in addition to the compensation awarded to the injured party.

Another facet reflects a different light. Every action, however damaging to the community, was brought at the instance of an individual. Those that were brought by the king were, for a long time after the Conquest, thought of as arising from wrongs against him personally, in a sense, if only as an attack on his majesty by a breach of his peace.

At the Conquest, William had available a military force capable of defeating any opposition in England. He had had the good fortune not only to overcome the English king Harold but to have done so when Harold had just conquered the great force of Danes under their king Harold Hardrada. William and his gang of warriors of

LAW AND ORDER: THE GROWTH OF THE CRIMINAL LAW

different nationalities, many of them mercenaries, were faced with new tasks of governing a conquered people. The English had only a poorly developed law of crime to offer. Its technology was insufficient for the demands of an occupying army. A criminal might suffer the dreadful sanction of communal society: ostracism. It is easy to be contemptuous of outlawry as a punishment and underrate its deterrent effect. It is certainly a sign of weakness of government that it could not keep offenders within its control and it has rightly been said that 'primitive law could not measure its blows.' But the effectiveness of outlawry can still be attested by the modern outcast who breaks the fundamental rules of the group, the blackleg who is sent to Coventry by his workmates or the Solzhenitsyn banished from his country. By the time of Edward I (1272–1307) an outlaw could no longer be killed like an animal by anyone who would and could, but by that time outlawry had ceased to be a punishment so much as a procedure to compel appearance in court.

The blood feud according to a statutory tariff seems crude now. The laws of the English kings were truly terrible but, as Potter says, 'It might be an eye for an eye or a tooth for a tooth, but it could not be an eye for a tooth.' Vengeance might still be private and fierce but its limits were fixed. And because it was fixed it was more easily commutable to the payment of a money compensation and consolation. A wrongdoer might have to pay *wer*, the price set out in the statutory tariff as appropriate to the status of criminal and victim; *wite*, the fine payable to the king; and *bot* or compensation for the wrong done. But some wrongs were bootless (*botleas*) and no *bot* money could buy the criminal off. Death for the criminal and forfeiture of his property were the punishments for those specially wicked crimes. Punishment was necessary to protect the community. The anti-social behaviour was not something which concerned only the parties. Where the king's interest was attacked, his rights were protected by pleas of the Crown. The more pleas of the Crown a king might have, the greater his sphere of interest.

William the Conqueror was not the first occupying foreigner. Canute had won for himself dominion over a large area of England and set out a list of crimes, varying from one part of England to another, which he claimed touched him directly, including not only violation of the king's peace and neglect of military service but also ambush and forcible entry into another's house. Canute also, it is said, required the community in which a dead body was found to prove that it was English and not Danish, by witnesses who swore to its parentage.

All these elements were used by the Norman kings to make the law they needed. They took over the Saxon system whereby the community was responsible to the central government for the behaviour of all the individuals who made it up. To this they added a technique they had learned in Normandy: the inquest. The king summoned to advise him a committee of men from the community in which the business to be transacted arose. These committees were called juries, but they were different from the old juries familiar to the Saxons, which had acted as 'oath-helpers', swearing that a party's oath was worthy of belief. They performed a quite different function from a modern jury, which listens to the evidence and decides guilt. 'Jury' originally meant no more than a group of men sworn in for some purpose. The king raised his jury by instructing his sheriff or some other officer to swear them in. When a body was found, and its killer was unknown, the king demanded a heavy fine from the local community unless a local jury would swear that the dead man was English, not Norman. The jury was called upon to make 'presentment of Englishry'.

DEVELOPMENT IN THE TWELFTH AND THIRTEENTH CENTURIES

By the time of Henry II (1154–89) the presenting jury was regularly used to deal with crime. The Assizes of Clarendon (1166) and Northampton (1176) — the word 'assize' in this sense means 'ordinance' — required the sheriff of each county to summon a jury from each hundred to present to royal commissioners the names of all people suspected of murder or theft. The presenting jury became known as the 'grand jury', which still exists in the United States. Its job was publicly to indict criminals, to bring them to justice. It played no part in the trial, which at that time was a simple appeal for a manifestation of divine judgment, known as 'the ordeal'.

The ordeal was the only available technique for testing guilt or innocence. There being no rational method of calling and assessing evidence, an appeal was made to God to decide. The priests had the necessary technology. The seriousness of the procedure was emphasized by the pain or terror inflicted, not as a punishment (because guilt had not yet been proved) but to make all concerned recognize the solemnity. The priest prepared a hot iron bar, which the accused must carry for 9 feet during Mass, or hot liquid for him to plunge his hand in. The injury was then bandaged. After three days the bandage was removed. If the wound was clean, the accused was adjudged not guilty — by God. If it had festered, God had pronounced guilt. There was a similar test in other courts in which the accused was bound and lowered into water near the church. The priest conjured up God's assistance. If the accused sank, God had found him innocent and an attempt was made to rescue and revive him. If he floated, God had made the water reject him and he was found guilty. For privileged accused, particularly priests, a more refined test was devised. The holy morsel of blessed bread was swallowed. If it choked the accused he was adjudged guilty — by God.

There were suspicions that the priests manipulated the proceedings to produce what they considered the right verdict. There must have been others who had equally little faith. Others started to argue that it was not quite proper to expect God to attend as a matter of legal routine. In any event, the Church at its Lateran Council in 1215 forbade priests to participate in ordeals, which quickly fell into disuse. There must always have been some uncertainty about the efficacy of the test because even if the accused 'came clean' from the ordeal, they were sent into exile. They had to 'abjure the realm' by going to the nearest port and taking ship.

The Assizes of Clarendon and Northampton dealt only with the great wrongs, murder and theft, and though their procedure of indictment by grand jury was extended to other crimes, it was not available to redress a private grievance. The process for that was the appeal of felony, the challenge to personal combat, self-help transformed into judicial process. Trial by battle was introduced by the Norman conquerors, at first as a privilege for Normans only, who were allowed to fight anyone who challenged their oath. In the thirteenth century the privilege was extended to both English and Normans, to defend themselves against not only the appeal of felony but the writ of right, described in Chapter 6.

The first part of an appeal of felony was heard in the thirteenth century by justices in eyre, royal inspectors skilled in both administrative and judicial techniques, as then still undifferentiated, who were sent to all parts of the realm. It was their duty to ensure that the tasks of government delegated to the local community had been properly carried out. The justices in eyre put to a presenting jury a set list of questions built up over the years, called the articles of the eyre, and sent them off to find out the answers. Meanwhile, those who had grievances and were eager to take advantage of the presence of skilled royal decision-makers, free at least from local bias, brought them to the justices of the eyre for decision, including appeals of felony.

When in 1215 the Church forbade the use of the ordeal, there was no means of trying those presented by grand juries. In 1218 Henry III (1216–72) put an end to the rebellion which had started in the last years of the reign of his father, John (1199–1216), and in reintroducing law and order had to deal with the prisoners awaiting trial. They were allowed to have their guilt decided by a jury of their neighbours. This petty jury, not the grand jury which had indicted them, decided the simple question of guilt or innocence. By this procedure the accused were said to 'put themselves upon the country'.

During the long reign of Henry III, there was still plenty of criminal work being done in courts outside the royal system. Within it, in addition to the new indictments, there were still appeals of felony. It became necessary for one who brought the appeal, an essentially private prosecution, in order to secure the assistance of the court in putting the accused in jeopardy of conviction of a capital offence, to allege an element in the accused's crime which was specially wicked. The crime had to be a felony, an act so bad or motivated by such malice that, like the bootless crimes of Saxon England, punishment was demanded for the good of the community.

Homicide was of course a crime and by the Statute of Gloucester 1278 juries were instructed to distinguish between a killing by accident, which was no felony, and killing by design, which was. Other felonies were suicide, wounding, grand larceny (where that which was stolen was worth more than a shilling), rape and arson. Felony was punished by hanging (or, if you were lucky, maiming) and forfeiture of land and goods. Treason was even more evil than the other felonies and needed specially frightful punishment.

Less wicked conduct might be punished as a breach of the peace, and an appeal of felony would usually be accompanied by an allegation of such a breach, to be fallen back on if the felony charge failed. The criminal element of such a breach was the progenitor of the misdemeanours: the civil element produced the tort of trespass. Misdemeanours, or criminal trespasses, were punished by what would now be called a fine (the amercement to the king) with imprisonment in default of payment. There was no tariff of length of imprisonment. As will be shown in Chapter 10, an amercement was payable to the king even on a civil trespass.

ASSIZES

When the eyre, the occasional visitation by government inspectors, could no longer cope with its work and got bogged down in one county perhaps for years at a time, more work fell to the justices who had been commissioned to hear the petty assizes. It must not be forgotten that their most important work, the assize of novel disseisin, though a way of testing ownership of land, was at first concerned with keeping the peace. The petty assizes acquired additional jurisdiction over the years from the start of the fourteenth century, sometimes general jurisdiction granted by statute. Commissions of gaol delivery instructed them to clear the gaols by bringing to trial those indicted and imprisoned. Commissions of oyer and terminer empowered them to hear and dispose of whatever work was specified in the commission as in need of attention. The Statute of Westminster II c. 30 (1285) and a statute of 14 Edward III (1340) gave assize judges powers which led to the *nisi prius* system. A case might be started in Westminster in the courts of King's Bench or Common Pleas and proceed to the stage where the verdict of a petty jury of the county was required to conclude it. It would then be adjourned to a later sitting of that court in Westminster unless before (*nisi prius*) that date it had been dealt with in the county by assize judges taking a jury's verdict there. The eyre passed away but the assize judges took over and performed essentially similar tasks until assizes were abolished in England just a few years ago in 1971.

JUSTICES OF THE PEACE

As the memory of occupation by foreigners faded, the need for military rule lessened. But the centuries of occasional and sometimes chronic unrest kept the need for peacekeepers. There were no police. There was not much of a standing army. Local magnates were concerned with order in the places they considered their responsibility. In time they were transformed into justices of the peace, the traditional unpaid glorified local landowners who were all the government working people would know in England before the industrial revolution. As Harding puts it, 'J.P.s ... were the landlords in another guise.' They used their judicial and local government powers in the special interests of themselves and the general interests of their class. Their class won power in the Commons and saw to it that their jurisdiction was extended by statutes of all kinds, not only dealing with crime, but trade and commerce, industrial relations, and (the matters which made them most hated) relief of the poor and protection of their game from poachers. They were led by the head peacekeeper, the quasi-military governor of the county, the Lord-Lieutenant.

The work of the justices of the peace was done either in the great county quarter sessions, held at Hilary, Easter, Midsummer and Michaelmas, or between times in petty sessions, held in districts into which the county was divided. The justices of the peace were to some degree under the supervision of the assize judges who visited twice a year and later of the Privy Council. They heard private petitions and submitted them to a grand jury who if satisfied presented the accused for trial on indictment. It was also possible for a trial to begin on an information from a private person who felt in some way encouraged to prosecute on behalf of the Crown, often because he had received a statutory payment for his informer's services. Not only a private person but also the king's attorney might lay an information.

HOMICIDE

The great advance of Saxon law was from feud to compensation, as uniform royal codes supplemented and reformed disparate customary laws. Most wrongs, even killings, could be bought off and tribal fighting avoided. Only crimes such as ambush, which struck so deep at law and order that society itself was threatened, were bootless. The Normans could leave no serious manifestation of disorder to be dealt with by composition and compensation. William had a bloody hand and well knew from successful experience in Normandy the advantages of terror. He also recognized the vulnerability of an occupying force. The system of presentment of Englishry required the community to pay a fine, called *murdrum*, on the unnatural death of a Norman. Every killing, even if accidental, was a matter for State intervention. All homicides were matter for the royal courts to deal with and gave rise to a plea of the Crown.

What was to happen, then, if a boy shot an arrow at a target and a careless stroller walked in the way of it? Could not the archer's youth, his noble purpose in preparing himself to defend his king and country, and the victim's folly be pleaded as defences? In 1256, a Shropshire jury found that an eight-year-old boy, who killed a man in this way, should be outlawed, and amerced his village for not presenting him.

The law of homicide grew from the exceptions which were necessarily created from the general rule that any killing was a crime. An inquest was held to find the cause of death. The jury might find that though the death was unnatural, the killer was not responsible. Though still convicted, the killer would be granted a royal pardon. The Crown would make no claim and impose no punishment. The family of the victim could bring an appeal of felony to recover compensation.

In addition to accident, self-defence became a ground for pardon. A distinction was drawn between one who had refused to participate in the violence until he must fight or risk death or serious injury, that is he had done what the court considered a reasonable man would do, and one who, while not starting the fight, had too enthusiastically responded to the challenge or the opportunity. The former would be pardoned. The latter was at first guilty of murder, later of manslaughter only. The distinction came to be drawn between killing in a sudden fight and premeditated murder. By statutes of 1390 and 1497, no pardons could be granted if there was 'malice aforethought'. 'Provocation' became a defence which reduced murder to manslaughter.

LARCENY

Theft was a simple wrongful taking of another's goods. Larceny is a rather more restricted notion, committed by taking goods intending to deprive the possessor of them permanently. Larceny was a felony punishable by death, but a distinction was made if the goods were worth less than a shilling. The sum was increased over the centuries. Theft of goods below that value was petty larceny and not a capital offence. The value of the goods was set by the jury which sometimes took the opportunity to avoid the death penalty by undervaluing them. The judge too might be moved by pity to declare that the thing stolen was not of its nature an object of larceny because, for example, it was land not goods.

TREASON

Governments are usually astute to suppress effective opposition from those they govern. A sign of progress is the provision of genuine safeguards for those who threaten a government's power. It is a paradox that the statute which defined the crime of treason, thereby seeking to delimit the crown's arbitrary repressive power, was to become a foundation of tyranny, available whenever it was considered expedient to crush opposition.

In 1350, when the Statute of Treasons was passed, the king was still concerned with his revenue from forfeiture and the statute went some way to restricting his power to kill as traitors those whose land he coveted. Only those were guilty of treason who 'compassed or imagined' the death of the king or his heir-apparent; or levied war against the king or assisted his enemies; or counterfeited his seals or money or imported false coin; or killed the king's chancellor or treasurer or judge in the performance of his duty.

Petty treasons were committed by those who killed their lord or husband or master or a bishop. Forfeiture was then to the lord and the punishment was death, not the barbarities reserved for high treason.

THE SUBSTANCE OF THE LAW

It is only in this century and the last that there has been an effective amelioration of the criminal law. Before, there was little humanitarian zeal to make conviction fairer or punishment less harsh. At the start of the nineteenth century death might be the penalty for more than two hundred felonies, including shoplifting, going bankrupt, consorting with gipsies or impersonating a Chelsea Pensioner. And death was not the severest pain: appalling torture and humiliation were reserved for high treason: the 'hanging, drawing and quartering' which involved among its unspeakable inhumanities the removal of the victim's guts, while alive, to be burnt before his face.

The great jurists like Lord Chief Justice Ellenborough, with the enthusiastic support of most of the bishops, fought successfully to delay reform. The appeal of felony was not formally abolished until 1819. It was only in the latter half of the last century that the prosecution of criminals became formally the responsibility of the Crown and practically the job of the police. Only in 1836 were prisoners given the right to address the court through counsel. Even that belated and inadequate recognition of a simple basic right was opposed by most of the judges.

REFERENCES AND FURTHER READING

Milsom, S.F.C., *The Historical Foundations of the Common Law* (Butterworths 2nd ed., 1981, hereinafter called Milsom and referable to all later chapters).

Turner, E.S., *Roads to Ruin: the Shocking History of Social Reform* (Michael Joseph, 1950; Penguin, 1966).

5. The Feudal System and the Administration of Justice

THE COURTS AFTER THE NORMAN CONQUEST

People in developed societies are used to thinking of the administration of justice as naturally the monopoly of a government. Not necessarily one central government. In Australia and the United States, for example, there are many governments and separate systems of law for each of the states and for the federation and its territories. A constitution allocates their respective jurisdictions. Between states the division is geographical: between federal government and states different powers are distributed.

Moreover, those who belong to religious communities may acknowledge the jurisdiction of ecclesiastical courts, sometimes with significant powers over their ordinary lives, as Catholic courts have over the dissolution of marriage or Islamic courts over succession on death. Those who still live in a communal society are used to at least two systems of law: the new law of a central administration and the customary law of their own group.

Yet even those who are used to such plurality will not find it easy to understand the diversity of legal systems in England after the Conquest. For one thing, the administration of justice was a privilege (like holding a market) shared by the powerful: not only the king but also the lord and the bishop, as it had been in Anglo-Saxon times. Indeed, the old Anglo-Saxon courts survived the Conquest for centuries: the local courts of shire and hundred, with jurisdiction both civil and criminal covered most matters of ordinary life for the great majority of people, though the ordinary people might take some of their disputes instead to manorial courts. They were still not courts in the restricted modern sense but meetings where many administrative matters were dealt with.

The Norman kings, like their Saxon forerunners, had their own courts, which did judicial jobs but also transacted a great deal of other business of the central government. In these meetings sat those who were traditionally part of the Court, in the social or political rather than any judicial sense, that is the courtiers: those who held high office of State and those others whom the king usually had about him.

LAW AS ADMINISTRATION

Like many successful military dictators who have come to power by conquest before and since, William the Conqueror pretended that his usurpation of the throne was lawful, that he was the rightful heir, and that his innovations were the mere repetition, reintroduction and reinforcement of the good old traditional customs and laws preserved in oral tradition. But his tasks were great. If he was to hold and enjoy his newly conquered country, he could not rely on his defeated foes to run it for him. But he could not start from scratch. Whether he liked it or not he had to make use of the institutions which the Anglo-Saxons provided, including the customary law which prevailed throughout the country, but varied from place to place. He had to secure control over all the land he claimed, and law and order were the tests of his rule. The king's peace of Saxon times came to have a different flavour for the defeated English.

The laws or customs, and the procedures for enforcing them, which William found on his arrival were probably more highly developed than those he left behind in Normandy but they were still predominantly communal and customary. The same jobs had to be done by local and central administration, but there were new ones too. In particular, the Norman kings, as colonial administrators, needed to keep an eye on what was going on.

That explains Domesday Book, started within twenty years of the Conquest, which lists owners and properties before and after 1066, a register arranged by counties, as the shires had come to be called, areas of land under the control of Norman warlords, or clergy, or English collaborators, all responsible to the king.

The courts of county and hundred were the instruments of royal administration. Each county court was controlled by the reeve of the county, the shire reeve or sheriff who was the king's man, with the king's authority and accountable to him. In the courts of hundred or *wapentake*, whether owned by king, or lord, or abbot, the presiding officer was the reeve or bailiff of the hundred who, whether servant of king or not, was an officer of the crown. Franchises to hold courts could be in the hands of men who were not royal officers, but they were always subject to the king's scrutiny which jealously restricted their jurisdiction.

THE NEW POWER STRUCTURE

What we think of as the feudal system in England was the legitimation and elaboration of the realities of conquest and military dictatorship. When William I, with his force of knights and other adventurers from Normandy, Flanders and elsewhere, defeated the English forces and conquered the whole of England, he had the political problems both of holding down the conquered English and of controlling his warlords, who necessarily had the military power not only to do that 'peace-making' job for him but to threaten his supreme command. They took their spoils too in the form of land, the only kind of income-producing capital then available. We shall see how the various manifestations of the sharing of the spoils developed: power, responsibility, property and privilege.

The control of an area of conquered land, necessarily taken from the conquered, cannot at first be described as property. That came later and slowly. But control demanded administrative machinery, which the old local courts of hundred and borough, shire and city did not comprehensively provide. The new rulers needed their own feudal courts to deal with disputes between themselves and with their workers. From the start there was a hierarchy, which lawyers (and other scholars) were later to try to make systematic and call the feudal system. But the picture of that complexity drawn by later commentators shows little more reality than the final score tells you of the struggle between players in a football match.

To survive you had to submit to the new power structure. If you were a great lord, you needed the approval of the king. The king, of course, needed the support of the great lords as a whole but could usually manage without any one of them. Safe in the confidence that he had royal favour, the great lord could grant his protection to his tenants. They would provide him in return with services of some kind. At first, most of them were fighters on horseback: the knights. The possibilities of further stages in this hierarchy and permutations of their nature were as considerable as they were natural, and always at the bottom were the agricultural workers, many unfree, who depended on some lord not only for 'protection' but also for the distribution of corporate resources (for example the strip system of dividing up the fields), perhaps seed, agricultural equipment, administration of co-operative systems and so on. In particular, though, there was a need for law and order of a kind that at least avoided resort to violence and self-help.

The king kept plenty of land himself, with no great lord between him and it, for his own direct support and pleasure, where he played the role taken elsewhere by the lord. At the lowest level, too, there would be land, called 'demesne land', which was worked by the workers of the manor directly for the lord. The manor became the typical economic unit, though county and hundred were the units (with the exceptional units such as city, borough and religious holding) of administration.

THE FEUDAL COURTS

It is not necessary to consider the complexities of all the many kinds of courts. Remembering that in theory every lord had the right and duty to hold a court or regular business meeting for his tenants, and that there was no system, but rather a struggle between the various jurisdictions, long drawn out and usually imperceptible, it is possible to classify the feudal courts, sometimes called 'seignorial' (or lords') courts, roughly into two groups.

The first, and more important in the long run, comprises the courts which lords of the manor held for their tenants. As the basic economic unit, the manor was a complex of customary rights and duties, concerning not only the allocation of agricultural tasks but also the limited rights of individuals to occupy land for use. Agricultural labourers would also look first to the manor court to resolve disputes against the lord of the manor himself. Eventually these rights became a kind of property, copyhold, which was made the equivalent of ownership, free from all customary impositions, only in 1925.

The other group is of courts at a higher level, where disputes between those who were lords themselves would be heard. If those lords held direct from the king, they were called 'tenants-in-chief' (*in capite*), and their dispute would be heard in the court of their lord, the king. If they were not, then in the court of whoever was their lord, where the court would be made up of the tenants of the superior lord, all of whom had the right or, as they saw it, the duty to attend and sit in judgment, on matters such as who was the legal heir, that is according to the oral customary law (which by then almost everywhere preferred the eldest son) and on the facts as they knew them. These were matters of great importance and of great interest to the king, who was usually just one step away and financially interested in the outcome. Eventually the matters within their jurisdiction fell more and more to be dealt with by the royal courts, and the common law (which the king's judges knew), the facts being found by a jury.

OTHER KINDS OF COURTS

There were many other kinds of courts in the twelfth century. Franchise courts were bought from or granted by the king. The travelling merchants had their own courts at the fairs, called 'courts of piepowder'. But the most important were the courts of the Church. Every citizen was a Christian, at least publicly so far as status was concerned. There were Jews from William the Conqueror's time until their extermination or expulsion by Edward I in 1290, but they were not treated as legal persons and needed the special protection of the king. Before the Conquest, ecclesiastical business was done in the lay courts, or rather in the administrative bodies, the courts of shire and hundred, which did not have their separate tasks differentiated as ecclesiastical or civil (any more than they were divided into administrative and judicial) until William I created separate ecclesiastical courts in 1072–6. When they adopted Roman procedure late in the twelfth century, it was too late for them to influence the lay courts of the central government greatly by their example, because by that time the lay courts had begun to work out their own professional practices. On the continent of Europe, however, that was not so and the civil courts of France and England to this day show that important historical distinction by their different procedures.

Civil and ecclesiastical jurisdictions were carefully demarcated from each other. The quarrels of Henry II (1154–89) and Archbishop Thomas Becket were yet to come and many of those who sat in lay courts, sometimes the majority of justices in the royal courts, were clergy. Yet the Church had jurisdiction then over many matters which, though they are now ordinary parts of the law's work, were slow to leave the ecclesiastical courts. Marriage and legitimacy, the proof of wills, even broken promises, were obviously matters for the Church. But jurisdictional disputes arose over how far these overlapped with the civil courts' unquestioned jurisdiction over dower and inheritance, contracts and property, which gradually extended as the Church courts lost their jurisdiction. Is a forsworn oath sacrilege or perjury? Can the sin of usury be pleaded as a defence to a claim for a debt? Which court decides? The division of jurisdiction depended on an uneasy compromise which an interfering Pope or an English religious reformer could disturb. The customary law was always conservative. The courts of equity, whose history is discussed in Chapter 8, were never Church courts.

THE EARLY DEVELOPMENT OF THE ROYAL COURTS

William the Conqueror was a brutally efficient military dictator. He had fought his way up from a hazardous childhood by being an adroit survivor and a more successful soldier than his competitors until he narrowly defeated Harold and added all England to his dominions, claiming it as rightfully his own. Under his domination, in the colony England, the old certainties were destroyed, however fervently he professed (in a foreign tongue) to preserve them. All power lay with the foreigner whose military strength had overturned the old order. New machinery for the exercise of power had to be devised and, as later chapters show, new systems of managing land.

Carefully avoiding trouble with the Church, buying its support by giving it new privileges, granting it jurisdiction over its own affairs and keeping its great men in his court, William I began to define his ambitions and lay down the foundations of his administrative structure. He used the office of sheriff as his first major tool, appointing his own Normans to the job. They were not the greatest of magnates, but landowners of importance nevertheless, whom he could control. He subjected them to the audits of his Exchequer, his taxing and accounting office. The king also used what were called 'justiciars'. Of all the terms which lead to an anachronistic anticipation of legal development, one of the most misleading is the confusion of *justiciarius* with judge. There was at first one justiciar who was the king's right hand man and deputy. He was viceroy when the king was not in England. He was head of the king's administration. Later, when there were several justiciars, the supreme offices fell to the Chief Justiciar. For a time there were justiciars appointed to sit in local courts but within a century after the Conquest those regional justiciars had served their function and disappeared.

They were superseded by what were called the 'justices in eyre', the *justiciarii totius Angliae* (justices of all England) whose job was not restricted to any region but who travelled anywhere in the kingdom where there was administrative work to be done. They shared the growing burden of government with the newly emerging royal courts. The sheriff became less of a judicial figure as the justiciars in eyre and those who sat in the courts at Westminster became more. The sheriff's job became to carry out the instructions in the letter the king sent him, the writ, in particular to make sure that defendants appeared before the court to face complaints against them.

The story of the growing supremacy of the royal courts is long and complex. Indeed its content is disputed by scholars. But its plot can be described simply if anachronistically as the nationalization of property: the centralization of administration by a royal takeover of work of all the courts. Direct expropriation was made impossible by the political realities masquerading under the colour of ancient custom just as now it is political realities rather than constitutions which protect privileges and property.

The method chosen by the Norman kings and their successors for centuries was to take over by competing, by offering what might not have been a very good product but what at least could be shown to be better than anything they would allow their competitors to offer. The royal courts made good use of their advantages: better and certainly more final resolution and disposition of conflicts, through much greater resources, in particular of trained and experienced public servants and of uniform, mostly written, law. There was no lack of corruption in the royal courts, where it was common to bribe judges until the seventeenth century, but at least a litigant could get away from local pressures of influence and corruption.

THE EYRE

One long lasting institution of royal justice was the eyre. The eyre was at first a technique of central government, a visitation from the king's personal representative. Henry II established fixed circuits and claimed for his justiciars exclusive jurisdiction over the major crimes. Punishments were savage: enough hanging and dismemberment, removing hands, feet, eyes or genitals to satisfy present day Saudi Arabia. Those who were visited by the eyre considered it a great imposition and protested to the king if it came round too often. Seven years became the minimum respite between eyres.

That period was too long to allow the eyres to do their jobs properly. Eyres were inquests rather than courts and inspected rather than judged. They audited and collected revenue and made sure that the lands of felons were forfeited to the king. But they also heard what today we would call civil disputes between subjects which did not concern the king's interests. They applied the local customary law but soon supplemented it with their own law which they made common to the whole kingdom. Later chapters will show how they introduced new legislative inventions such as the possessory assizes and trials on indictment. Audits may wait for seven years but litigants do not believe that the resolution of their conflicts can.

The importance of efficient, honest, available courts was recognized. Some of Magna Carta's more resounding phrases are those by which the king promised (in 1215): 'To no one will we sell, to no one will we refuse or delay rights or justice'; 'We will appoint as justices, constables, sheriffs or bailiffs only such as know the law of the kingdom and really mean to observe it; and to hold a royal court at a fixed place.'

At first the king travelled all over the realm. A military leader of an occupying force needs to check up all the time himself as well as send his representatives to snoop around for him. On the other hand, the king was often not in England, his newly conquered colony, but at home in Normandy.

THE *CURIA REGIS*

All developments of central royal justice can be traced to the body of men who were physically close to the king, the *curia regis*. It is best not to think of the curia in the eleventh and twelfth centuries as a court at all, because it is so difficult to avoid the echoes of modern courts and procedure, and hear the true voices of courtiers. It is even useful to think of *curia regis* as the king's gang, his henchmen and hangers on. And as there is no definite article in

Latin, *curia regis* does not always mean *the* king's court. It is just as likely to mean *a* king's court.

Yet by 1300 there was a system of royal courts with professional judges, lawyers, properly kept records and professional books, dispensing a common law (much of it based on new reforming legislation) which was well known in those courts and quite sophisticated if limited in scope.

Looking back, it is easy to see that there were different jobs to be done. How easy it is now to suppose that they were put into categories and neatly allotted to different departments of a judicial system. It was not like that. There were, first of all, plenty of courts already: the courts outside the central royal system which did the great bulk of the legal work until the sixteenth century, applying customary law from oral tradition and only gradually accepting the new common law. Every royal innovation was jealously scrutinized and often opposed by those whose source of income or privilege it infringed.

SEPARATION OF THE ROYAL COURTS

One of the delights of the detective historian is to find in the surviving sources the earliest mention of an institution. If it is clear that in 1500 there are three separate courts which have for a very long time been called in Latin *coram rege*, *in banco* and *ad scaccarium*, and are by 1500 translated 'King's Bench', 'Common Pleas' and 'Exchequer', how exciting to trace back these Latin terms as far as possible, assuming that the discovery of the terms in the sources of earlier centuries will illustrate the existence of the same institution, though of course at an earlier stage of development! Historians, however, are smarter than that and have recognized that those Latin terms started off by describing no such institutions. They were primarily geographical: they pointed out the place where sat a group of the king's officials drawn from the *curia regis*. By the twelfth century, groups of members of the curia might do their work in any of those places. *Coram rege* means 'in the presence of the king'. The group *coram rege* sat in the king's presence, not necessarily always with the king physically among them, but at least at the place where he was. Necessarily they were drawn from those closest to the king, who travelled with him wherever he went. For the purposes of doing justice in England, this group could not function when the king left the realm.

The group *ad scaccarium* met at a place called the exchequer, the king's treasury and tax office. They had decent accommodation and confusion has been caused to historians because the other groups sometimes used it. *In banco* means no more than at a place called 'the bench'.

It is hardly surprising that in time the divisions became more formal and came to deal with different kinds of work. The Bench (which was not the forerunner of King's Bench) emerged from the *curia regis* in this way. A statute of 1178 says that five *justiciarii* were to remain at a place called *curia regis*. For nearly half a century, at the crucial formative time, England had kings who spent most of their time abroad. In the second half of the twelfth century, Henry II and Richard I were distracted from their English responsibilities by the affairs of their other kingdom or the Crusades. The great pioneer of English legal scholarship, Glanvill, writing around 1187, showed that there were different groups of judges *in banco* and *ad scaccarium*. Both were resident at Westminster for various reasons of administrative necessity, all were members of the same team of officials and if the king was present they were the *curia regis coram rege*.

When King John (1199–1216) made his permanent headquarters in England in 1209, all the work was done *coram rege* and the Bench fell into disuse. John liked to keep an eye on everything himself and he obviously enjoyed judging. Even when he could not physically be present, he preferred the fiction that he was, and his court sat *coram rege* rather than *in banco*. But Magna Carta in 1215 (Chapter 17) ordained effectively that permanent provision should be made for common pleas to be heard in a fixed place, which came to be Westminster Hall. Common pleas were those disputes which did not involve the king's interests. This for the first time showed what was to be a distribution of work, a demarcation of jurisdiction. The court *in banco* would hear common pleas: the court *coram rege* would have jurisdiction only over pleas of the Crown and trespasses involving breaches of the king's peace. The categories were not exclusive at that date, however, and the overlap became much disputed later on.

The interfering and suspicious John had caused Bench to fall into disuse but, on his death soon after Magna Carta, the infancy of his successor Henry III made it impossible for the court *coram rege* to work. Because the king was a child, he could not take part in judging. The Bench revived and flourished and when the court *coram rege* began to sit again, the division between them was final and recognized. By 1234 the two divisions had separate records; their membership no longer overlapped; by 1272 each had its own chief justice. Still they were known by their Latin names. When they came to have settled English equivalents, confusion arose. By 1500 the court *coram rege* was known as King's Bench. The Bench needed a new name to distinguish it and found one in the nature of the actions which came before it: first Common Bench, later the Court of Common Pleas.

Naturally most work fell to the Bench (the Common Pleas). Some kinds of action were always within its jurisdiction alone, particularly those on the older writs. It shared trespass, even trespasses involving breaches of the king's peace, with King's Bench. It had the lion's share of work, the other royal courts of King's Bench and Exchequer being restricted to more specialized jurisdictions. The Court of Common Pleas became highly professional, with its chief justice and three judges always drawn from the serjeants-at-law who had a monopoly of pleading there. Most Year Books, described more fully in Chapters 13 and 14, were notes taken of its proceedings, perhaps in some cases by, and some probably for the use of, the student apprentices who sat in court and were a part of the brotherhood of professionals. But to start an action in the Court of Common Pleas a plaintiff needed to buy the right form. And the place which provided them was the royal secretariat: the Chancery.

The court which sat in the exchequer, the Exchequer of Pleas as it became known, concerned itself with government accounting and tax collecting, to which jurisdiction it had been limited by Magna Carta. It was efficient and unambitious until the struggle for work between King's Bench and Common Pleas whetted its appetite in the sixteenth century.

REFERENCES AND FURTHER READING

Harding, A., *The Law Courts of Medieval England* (George Allen and Unwin, 1973).
Van Caenegem, R.C., *The Birth of the English Common Law* (Cambridge U.P., 2nd ed, 1988).

6. The Writ System and the Forms of Action

WRITS

Writs are written documents, letters from the king. They were important from Saxon times as tools of administration. There are early examples which are not intended to lead to a judicial inquiry. They merely instruct the wrongdoer or, if he refuses, the sheriff to restore to a complainant land which the king states belongs to the complainant and the wrongdoer wrongly occupies. Later examples tell the sheriff to inquire into the facts and do what he finds right. Then the form becomes an instruction to the sheriff to command the defendant to do right or appear before the king's justices to give reasons for not doing what the court assumes is right, because the plaintiff said so. In this way the royal judges took jurisdiction from communal courts but still could offer no alternative to the customary law.

At first after the Conquest writs had no set form. They did not all go to the sheriff. They were drafted to suit the immediate and particular purpose for which they were needed. This means that at that time a writ was no more than an official government letter. But the natural tendency of the administrator is to save time by providing forms when there is enough demand for written documents of a kind. The clerks in the Chancery provided such forms. They were necessarily hand written, for no other technology was available. But some writs were provided according to well-known formulas. They were the *brevia de cursu*, the 'writs of course', written out by clerks called 'cursitors'.

Many complaints were made which did not fit these forms, for which writs were still specially drafted. Furthermore, many actions until the time of Edward III (1327–77) were begun without a writ of any kind, by a mere *querela* or informal complaint or bill. But from that time it became the general rule that you needed a writ to start an action in the king's common law courts at Westminster, though not in the local courts or before justices in eyre and never in Chancery. There was an interesting exception in King's Bench.

Because the court *coram rege* could always hear complaints without a writ in the county where it happened to be sitting, and because Westminster was in Middlesex, when King's Bench settled at Westminster it remained possible for a litigant in that county to start an action before it without a writ. And because the procedure was attractive, fictions were employed to extend its availability. They are described in Chapter 12. A legal fiction is a pretence, in which the court insists everyone must join, whereby the truth is concealed so that some difficulty, usually procedural, can be avoided in the interest of justice.

The king's letter was usually addressed to the sheriff of a county, instructing him to ensure that the defendant appeared, usually before a royal court, to answer the charges brought against him by the plaintiff. If the defendant did not appear to answer the charges, he was guilty of contempt of the king's writ and could be imprisoned. The nature of the complaint was set out briefly in the writ, usually according to one of the formulas. The plaintiff's lawyer, well versed in these formulas, would fit his client's claim to match the one he thought most appropriate, according to the facts which the client alleged. One of the Chancery clerks would issue the writ, authenticated by the great seal. That did not mean, however, that the right writ had been chosen. The first task of the defendant's counsel was to persuade the court that the writ was not appropriate to the claim. The court might quash the writ either because it was not the one which fitted the alleged facts, or because, if it was not a writ *de cursu*, it was an unacceptable innovation. If the court considered that the claim should have been brought on a different kind of writ, the plaintiff would lose similarly. Even if the court upheld the writ, the plaintiff could still lose if unable to prove the facts, on the evidence as we would now say. The plaintiff would then be liable to pay a fine to the king, to be amerced, 'to be in mercy for a false claim'.

Different writs had their different procedural advantages and drawbacks. A great deal of the lawyers' craft was a command of the learning about writs. They kept their own set of precedents — many still do — and the law books were based on the categories of writs, or forms of action. Your client, Martha, might tell you that her neighbour Matthew refused to hand back goods which belonged to her. An old action, one which had been created early in the history of the common law like detinue, might give Matthew the right to wage his law, to make proof depend on his word against

Martha's, solemnly sworn and supported by oath-helpers. A newer action, like trover, might have a more modern procedure, with a jury to decide on disputed facts. By manipulating the matter presented to you by your client, you might be able to choose the form of action more advantageous to her. The method of proof would not be the only consideration, though. You would have to consider whether the form of action gave your client the most expeditious and efficient method of enforcing her claim if the court accepted its validity. One form of action might allow the successful plaintiff to seize the goods of the defendant and have them sold to pay the amount awarded in the judgment. Another might allow the plaintiff to have the defendant arrested and imprisoned until the judgment debt was paid.

In advising a client, therefore, you would have to consider:

1. Was there a writ to fit the complaint? If there was no *breve de cursu*, could the Chancery clerk be persuaded to make one up? If not, could some other kind of process be used, perhaps a petition to the king or his chancellor? Would an action in a local court serve the purpose better?
2. If more than one writ was available, which form of action would suit your client's interest best? Usually the more modern would have a more modern technology.

As one would expect, there were some periods when it was easier to get writs made to measure, others when restrictions were imposed and plaintiffs kept within the known formulas.

The judges may have started to refuse to create new categories of writs because the barons and other owners of courts were concerned that otherwise the jurisdiction of the king's courts would be further extended and would swallow up the last of theirs. The Provisions of Oxford 1258 forbade the creation of new kinds of *brevia de cursu*, writs 'of course', without the agreement of the king in his council, that is without parliamentary approval.

No doubt the lords hoped by this measure, treated by the king as rebellious and not of statutory effect, to control what they considered to be, in modern terms, expropriation of their property without compensation. Though Bracton in his majestic treatise on the laws and customs of England, written at the same time, said, 'There will be as many formulas for writs as there are kinds of action', he would have been more (though not completely) accurate if, given the gift of prophecy, he had written, 'There will be only the kinds of action for which there are formulas for writs.' Few new writs were invented after 1258; as Bracton went on to say, 'for no one may sue without a writ, since without a writ the other is not bound to answer.' The general rule became, at least in common law courts, 'no remedy without a writ'. Writing had become the all-important technology of the common law. It was no longer possible to get your defendant before the king's court on an oral complaint alone.

If the Chancery clerks were forbidden to help the development of the law by making writs to measure, it was up to the judges to find ways of meeting new needs. If the categories of writs could not be multiplied, the judges would have to extend the scope of the existing ones. They did this in different ways, bringing all kinds of conflicts on new sets of facts within the old formulas, sometimes by fictions and sometimes by winking at technical requirements. The modern law with its substantive rules grew out of the reasons given by the judges for these extensions, the reasons they gave for deciding that the facts of the case before them fell (or did not fall) within the writ on which the plaintiff brought the action. And the judges' reasons were written down, collected, and made available to lawyers, first in the Year Books and then in their successors, the law reports, as is explained in Chapter 14.

The action of ejectment illustrates the process well. To understand that process it is necessary to see how disputes about ownership of land developed. Not until Chapter 7 will the growth of the land law be considered, but the substance of the old forms of action and their development must now be outlined.

WRITS OF RIGHT

The early writs show many examples of the form beginning with the word *Praecipe*, 'Command!'. After the usual formal address to the sheriff: 'The King to the sheriff of — shire, greeting,' it might go on: 'Command Luke that justly and without delay he give back to John [land briefly described] which John claims to be his right and inheritance etc.'

The writ, directing simply that land should be restored to its rightful owner, was called a 'writ of right'. If the plaintiff held the land directly from the king, he was a tenant-in-chief, *in capite*, and the writ was a *praecipe in capite*. If the plaintiff held of some intermediate lord, then the king directed the lord to do right to his tenant. If the writ were not for the restoration of land (or rather 'inheritable property' as technically defined) but for other property such as goods, then the appropriate writ of right was a writ of debt, or sometimes detinue.

These writs of right, then, instructed the sheriff to see that the defendant did right or came before the king's justices. If the plaintiff complained not of an infringement of a right but of a wrong done, the writ was not prepared to give the defendant the chance to put things right by some arrangement out of court. The action complained of was something that affected the king, analogous to a crime, perhaps a breach of the king's peace. If it was not, what concern was it of the central government? Let some other court deal with it, according to customary law. In particular, royal government was concerned to stop squabbles over land, and to resolve them by judicial means and prevent feuding. Whatever rights there were in land arose, in every case, from a grant made or endorsed by the king or one of his tenants, directly or indirectly. Land rights were not matters which could be left to private violence or self-help. That they should be dealt with in a proper and peaceful way was the fundamental requirement of good government. The right way was to hold an inquiry and see whether peaceful possession had been recently disturbed. This would deal with the immediate problem. Whoever had the better right to the land could then be dealt with in the more leisurely traditional way appropriate to such a refined legal problem.

NOVEL DISSEISIN

The immediate problem, though about property, was first seen as a threat to law and order, almost like a criminal matter today. It was a matter for an assize, a jury of 12 neighbouring men, who might well be supposed to be able to answer from their own knowledge the two questions posed to them:
1. Had the defendant unjustly and without a judgment 'disseised' (dispossessed in a technical way) the plaintiff?
2. Had this been done recently (the period was fixed according to a technical formula)?

If the assize answered no to either, the plaintiff lost: if yes to both, he was put back in possession. This procedure, the assize of novel disseisin, was created about 1166 and was well developed by the end of the thirteenth century. It was possessory, being concerned only with the claim to possession. Rights still had to be tried by the old writ of right, where the defendant had the opportunity of trial by battle.

A further division was into real and personal actions. The distinction is still of fundamental importance in the common law because property is still divided into the two categories fixed by that distinction: real and personal. Real property is property which could have been recovered only in a real action. That this division is accidental can be seen from the categories used by legal systems other than the common law, which usually have a distinction depending upon the physical nature of the property, movable or immovable.

There could be no 'disseisin', no dispossession sufficient for the assize of novel disseisin, unless the plaintiff could show 'seisin', a special kind of possession. The holder of a lease, even for 999 years, was not seised and therefore could not bring an assize of novel disseisin, still less a writ of right, if dispossessed. For this reason to this day leasehold property is personal property not real property. When realty passed on death to the heir and personalty to the next-of-kin, freehold land went to the former, leasehold to the latter.

And so, in theory, right was tried by the old writs of right and the assize of novel disseisin dealt with recent dispossession. Both of these were real actions and appropriate for disputes arising about freehold land. Moreover, there was a rule that if an action could be brought on an existing writ, no new writ was available. But a claim brought in one of the old real actions became unattractive. Their procedures were recognized to be antique and cumbersome. A way was found for a most unlikely substitute, by way of another legal fiction.

EJECTMENT

The action of trespass was concerned not with rights at all but with the need to redress a wrong so that law and order would be maintained. It had a handy and efficient technology, but what use was that to someone who wanted to assert title to land? Trespass lay for the wrong of forcible interference with the plaintiff's person, goods or land. In the case of land, trespass lay for the forcible interference with the plaintiff's possession. Trespass was an action for damages. How could this unlikely weapon help a plaintiff who wanted the court to assert ownership of the land? How could trespass be used to recover the land itself? Of all paradoxes in the development of the common law, the oddest is that the most efficient method of trying the title to freehold land was made possible by the clever manipulation of the law of leases.

The relation of lessor and lessee was at first purely personal; as we should say now, just a matter of contract between them. If the lessor evicted the lessee before the term was up, the lessee could sue the lessor for breach of the contractual duty. But that was in an action which lay only against the lessor. What if the lessor transferred the ownership of the leased land to a purchaser who turned the lessee out? From about 1237, the lessee had the action *quare ejecit infra terminum*, to make a purchaser from the lessor who had evicted the lessee answer 'why he had ejected him within the term of the lease.' By this writ the lessee, who had of course no 'real' action, could recover the land for the rest of the lease's term. This writ was available against those who were assignees from the lessor, not against other trespassers who turned the lessee out. Probably in the time of Edward II (1307–27) the lessee acquired the writ *de ejectione firmae*, 'about the ejection from the land holding', against anyone who evicted the lessee, but this action's remedy was damages only, not a return to possession. It was not until the middle of the fifteenth century that a lessee could use *de ejectione firmae* to recover possession. Then the lessee had the necessary weapon, a writ good against any dispossessor, by which to regain possession.

During the sixteenth century, lawyers adapted this efficient leaseholder's protection so that it could be used to try title to freehold land. They called the action simply 'ejectment'.

By the eighteenth century the real actions were obsolete. Ejectment, a remedy invented to protect leaseholds, the least interest in land, had become the regular method of protecting the greatest. Ejectment became the action by which ownership of freehold land was decided, despite its complicated fictions, because it was more efficient.

It worked like this. Alan wanted to prove his title to Blackacre and to get the court to recognize him rather than Maud as owner. Alan purported to lease the land to Guy, purely for the purposes of the action. Guy would try to take possession of the land under his lease and, if he was ejected, would bring an action of ejectment against the occupier Maud who had ejected him. To deal with this action, the court had to decide whether Alan had a right to create the lease, which only an owner had. Maud would have to deny Alan's title in order to justify her ejectment of Alan's lessee Guy.

By the start of the eighteenth century Alan was able to operate the mechanism of the action of ejectment by the use of fictions which the court would not allow the defendant to challenge. No real lease to a real lessee was required. Alan alleged that he had leased Blackacre to a make-believe character called regularly and unimaginatively John Doe, who had been ejected by an equally imaginary ejector, usually called Richard Roe, who was alleged to be the lessee of the real defendant Maud.

This dummy ejectment had the great advantage that it required not only no real leases but, more important, no real entry and no actual ejectment. Alan controlled the whole drama until Maud was forced to accept the fictions and assert her ownership. Maud was only allowed to defend her title if she agreed to pretend that the fictions were real.

Ejectment is this form seems to us comically unreal and clumsy. But it worked well and much better and more cheaply and simply than the only alternatives, the old real actions. That is why, though the fictions were abolished more than a century ago, the rules worked out in the action of ejectment are still used to prove title where it is not yet based on a register.

THE CHILDREN OF TRESPASS

There were other clever developments like ejectment but they were not enough to provide the machinery to cope with the new demands. The writ system could not satisfy even the needs of the society in which it developed, which had few potential litigants, an unsophisticated technology and a social structure which changed slowly. It broke down under the pressures of commerce and trade, the growing size and power of the bourgeoisie and the incipient industrial revolution.

The great breakthrough came like ejectment out of trespass, that 'fertile mother of actions' in Maitland's words. Developed from trespass was the action on the case. Unlike a writ of trespass, the writ of trespass on the case set out the particular facts on which the case was founded and thereby it broke through the restrictions of the formulas of the older writs. Trespass was about wrongs which infringed law and order. The writ of trespass recited that the wrong had been done 'by force of arms and against the peace of our Lord the King.' Case required no such allegations to be pleaded. Trespass lay only for direct wrongs, for positive acts. Case eventually came available when the wrong complained of was no more than an omission or failure.

Out of this escape-hatch from the sinking writ system sprang new categories which for a while developed as the early writs had done in their youth. Case became divided into well-known classes, analogous in a way to the *brevia de cursu*, called actions on the case 'in common form', such as 'trover' and *assumpsit*, with a catch-all category for the miscellaneous leftovers 'the action on the special case'. These are all considered in detail in Chapters 10 and 11.

It has been assumed since the end of the Middle Ages at the latest that the Statute of Westminster II 1285 had a lot to do with the later development of the forms of action. Its second chapter, called *in consimili casu*, provided that 'when in one case a writ is found and in like case, falling under like law and requiring like remedy, is found none, the clerks of Chancery shall agree to make a writ.' The meaning of those words is disputed but, whatever they mean and whether or not they will sustain the meaning given to them as the genesis of the action on the case, it has certainly been assumed since the sixteenth century that those words were the statutory origin of that form of action from which developed so much of our modern law of contract and tort described in Chapters 10 and 11. At first the action on the case was anomalous and lay only where no other writ was available, but before long this requirement lapsed and case became an alternative.

From case developed the modern law of contract through one of the common forms, assumpsit; the modern law of torts grew mainly out of the innominate action on the special case. The modern principles were fashioned by the judges in the reasons they gave why an action would lie or not.

The forms of action were abolished piecemeal in the nineteenth century. The process was completed by the Common Law Procedure Acts 1852 and 1854 and the Judicature Acts 1871–3. Yet the old categories and much of the old terminology remain. It is neither necessary nor indeed now possible to bring an action in one form rather than another. Yet later chapters will show that the modern law of property, contract and tort cannot be understood without a knowledge of the development of the forms of action. And it still matters that you know when to bring an action in damages and when in debt.

Maitland said, 'The forms of action we have buried, but they rule us from their graves.' It is still as much a half truth now as it was when it was said. Students who find the forms of action difficult to comprehend and are tempted not to bother with understanding them should look at the modern law to see how important they still are. At least they will discover that the forms of action still influence the divisions of their curriculum and the vocabulary of practice.

REFERENCES AND FURTHER READING

Maitland F.W., *The Forms of Action* (Cambridge U.P., 1941).

7. Property: its Invention and Protection

THE FEUDAL SYSTEM

Wealth is power, stored like electricity in a battery. The extent of the power that can be kept in this way varies from one society to another. In some the range is great, extending to all kinds of privilege and patronage. There are limits: no private armies, no bribery at elections, no unsubtle purchase of honours. And, of course, 'money can't buy me love', though some of the expensive fakes are notoriously hard to detect. Some of the things which remain in our realm of commerce are outside it in other kinds of society: the control of the media; the working time of other people; health, education, security and legal services.

Immediately after the Conquest, power lay with the new king and his barons. They had won it in battle and could keep it by military force. As they settled down first as an occupying army and then with their collaborators as the nobility and gentry, they carved up all the power among themselves, except for the privileges granted to the Church and the subordinate powers that belong to the farmworker and craftsman and trader from the irreducible relation they have with the realities of nature and production and exchange.

Earlier chapters have shown how the Norman kings and their successors, as quickly and comprehensively as possible, covered the nakedness of that military control with the trappings of civil power, through a system of administration which concentrated on keeping the peace. In that way England was given strong central government and became an effective State. In modern societies, rights are enforced by the State. Wealth in a capitalist society is largely made up of these State-enforced rights, typically the benefit of contracts: shares in or loans to that creature of the State, the limited liability company; contractual arrangements with banks, workers, customers, suppliers, insurers; speculative contracts with dealers in commodities or rights; and a multitude of other devices whose range is constrained only by the limits of the ingenuity of entrepreneurs and their financial and legal advisers.

THE IMPORTANCE OF LAND

In feudal times too there were of course chattels and cash and debts and bonds, workshops and monopolies and contracts for the future supply of goods and services. But wealth as a battery of power lay in land. With the ownership of land went status and security, privileges of all kinds in this world and even some hopes of advancement in the next. The history of the English law of property in land is the story of the breakdown of feudal relationships and, in their stead, the development and elaboration of new methods of exercising power over and through land: methods of transferring land and restricting the power to transfer it; of leaving land by will and forbidding wills of land; of carving up the rights in land into new forms and striking some down as illegitimate; of creating devices that would control the power over and enjoyment of land for generations and of schemes and fictions to escape those controls; and of whatever for the time being was effective to avoid contemporary equivalents of taxes and death duties.

It is commonplace for legal historians to describe a feudal system of landholding with elaborate legal machinery to protect it. Yet feudal society must have been on the wane when the system was centrally administered and required the royal courts and a common law to enforce it. When military power was all that was needed and all that there was to determine the ownership of land, then relations between king and lord, and lord and man, were direct and based on obvious immediate needs: the king's power to protect his lords and his need of their military support, and the same for lord and knight. All this, of course, had to rest on the production of food and other necessaries by agricultural labourers, free or serf.

But when the fighting stops many new possibilities open. Keeping the outward appearance of a feudal apparatus, the common lawyers sophisticated the simple but multifarious power relations of feudal realities until they created the complex and subtle machine they needed for post-feudal societies. Through the agrarian and industrial revolutions, through capitalism in its youthful vigour, mature development and metamorphosis into the welfare state and beyond, the system of property law has proved adaptable and useful. It is with us still and proves resilient to the attempts of reformers to see it off. Moreover its concepts have become constraints in countries which have never known feudalism and had a quite different language of property relations.

PROPERTY: ITS INVENTION AND PROTECTION   53

In communal societies, indeed in many post-feudal as well as earlier societies, land ownership is allodial; land is and was owned by individuals or groups such as clans absolutely, with no need to show the relation to a lord or king. Since the Norman Conquest, however, all land in England has been held directly or indirectly of the king. In the legal theory of the common law, no landowner is more than a tenant, who has not absolute ownership but an estate in the land. For centuries, those who claim to own land have been required to show by what written title (*quo warranto*) they hold it. And feudal realities required that land should not be owned by the clan but by individuals, on whose death it would pass to the eldest son.

A Modern Rationalization of Tenures

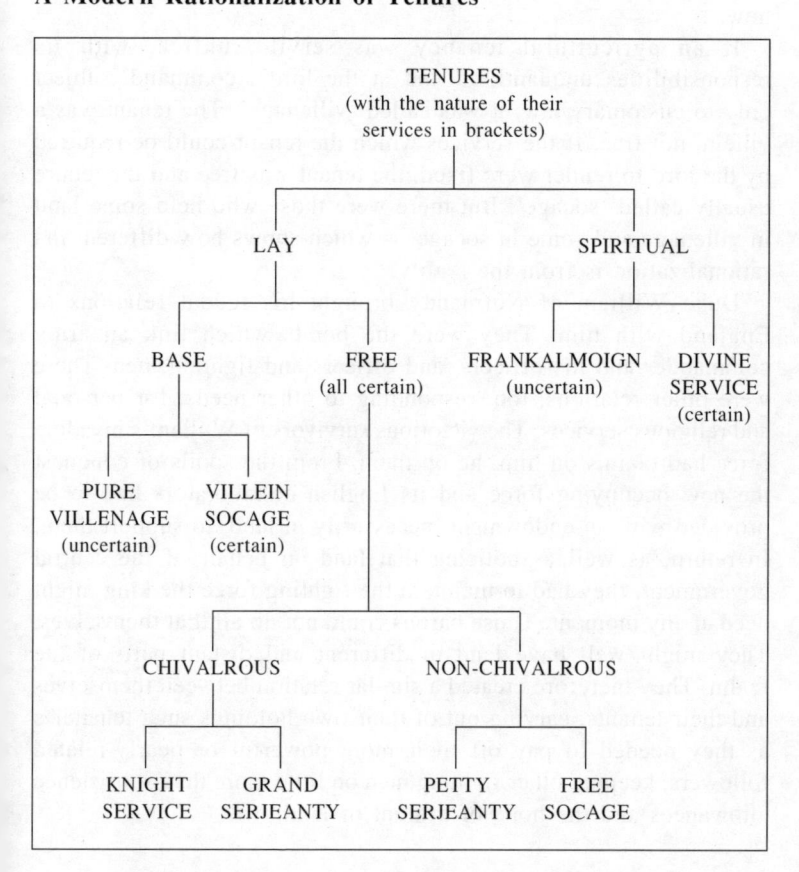

```
                        TENURES
                (with the nature of their
                   services in brackets)
                ┌──────────────┴──────────────┐
               LAY                         SPIRITUAL
        ┌───────┴───────┐             ┌───────┴───────┐
       BASE            FREE      FRANKALMOIGN      DIVINE
                   (all certain)   (uncertain)     SERVICE
                                                  (certain)
    ┌────┴────┐
   PURE     VILLEIN
 VILLENAGE  SOCAGE
 (uncertain) (certain)
        │
   ┌────┴────┐              ┌──────┴──────┐
CHIVALROUS              NON-CHIVALROUS
   │                          │
┌──┴──┐                    ┌──┴──┐
KNIGHT  GRAND            PETTY    FREE
SERVICE SERJEANTY      SERJEANTY  SOCAGE
```

LORD AND MAN

It is usual to look at feudal landholding from the top down: ownership granted by the king to a lord, lords to their tenants, with peasants farming the land. The common law concentrates its student's attention on the law in the king's courts and therefore on the estates in which the king had an interest. This was new law created after the Conquest to fit new needs. The landholding of those who produced the crops was customary, protected in the court of the agricultural worker's lord and was to some degree subject to the lord's discretion, if not manipulation. This customary law may have been little changed by the coming of the new Norman overlords. It certainly lasted longer than much of the law concerning the higher landholdings, some traces remaining until 1925 in England and faintly elsewhere even now.

If an agricultural tenancy was servile, unfree, with its responsibilities unquantified and at the lord's command, subject only to customary law, it was called 'villenage'. The tenant was a villein, not free. If the services which the tenant could be required by the lord to render were fixed, the tenant was free and the tenure usually called 'socage'. But there were those who held some land in villenage and some in socage — which shows how different the rationalization is from the reality.

Duke William of Normandy brought his feudal relations to England with him. They were the bonds which link an army commander and his officers, and officers and fighting men. There were other relations, too, responding to other needs, for personal and religious services. The victorious survivors of William's invading force had claims on him, he on them. From the spoils of conquest the new occupying force and its English collaborators had to be provided with an endowment, necessarily in land, to support them. In return, as well as policing that land on behalf of the central government, they had to maintain the fighting force the king might need at any moment. Those barons could not do all that themselves. They might well have land in different and distant parts of the realm. They therefore created a similar relation between themselves and their tenants, carving out of their own holdings such tenancies as they needed to pay off their more powerful or nearly-related followers, keeping other fighting men on little more than subsistence allowances and the hope of a grant of land.

This process, which we now call 'subinfeudation', might continue through more stages, each taker of land, tenant of his lord, making himself a lord by creating a tenant of part of his land, rather than by selling all or part of the land, which he could not at first do, having no property in it to sell but only rights of occupation and use. The relation of king to lord, or lord to man, was personal to them. More a relation of status than of contract, it was not yet sufficient to give the tenant property rights. The lord had a duty to safeguard the person of his man and protect his enjoyment of the land he had made him tenant of. The man's duty was to fight as well. Lord and man swore to each other the most solemn oaths of homage and fealty, in order to secure the performance of their mutual obligations.

Fighting prowess is a personal attribute. While a lord might be satisfied with an arrangement by which he granted enough land to keep Sir John in a condition to turn out when requested to join the lord's fighting force, he might think very little of the valour of Sir John's son, especially if he were a child, and still less of Sir John's widow or daughter. This simple relation of lord and man must at first therefore have been, and have been intended to be, for the joint lives of lord and man, at most. It had to end on the death of either.

The death of the lord had little importance once his part of the compact ceased to have substantial obligations, which it did once the central government took responsibility for law and order. The landholding was the pay which the lord gave the tenant for his services and it mattered little who was paymaster, lord or lady or infant, fighter or fop or abbot.

But what was to happen on the death of the tenant? Tenants were well aware of the problem and took from their lords promises to allow the land to pass to their heirs. The lord granted the land to the tenant and his heirs. The tenant had the land for his life. On his death his heir took it for life, and so on. This must have been the understanding at first. The lord could make certain demands when his tenant died but he could not break his promise to admit his tenant's heir. The lord's power to dispose of the land free of the claims of his tenant dwindled with the rise of the right to inherit. Instead he made other claims, called 'incidents', which in their turn lost their economic importance for all lords other than the greatest of lords, the king.

SERVICES

The lord granted land to the tenant as an endowment of capital to produce income to sustain the tenant so that he could render to the lord the service appropriate to his tenure. That is the feudal theory. If ever that was what really happened, it certainly did not happen for long. There was no system to be seen by contemporaries. The reality had become too complicated within a century of the Conquest. Not all holdings could be neatly classified as knight service or serjeanty or socage. A glance at the anachronistically schematic representation on page 53 shows for example that free socage and villein socage look very much alike. Those categories are at best crude, but a more detailed description would show not less but greater difficulties of categorization. One man's holding might be by a mixture of services. Another might hold different tenancies by different kinds of services, in knight service from one lord, in socage from another. In addition women could hold, inherit and even trade in land.

Moreover the exaction of services became impracticable. If the theory was to be believed, the tenancy was personal, it could neither be sold nor inherited. That would have been socially unacceptable and disruptive. Yet a knight might well be succeeded by an infant or a woman or have granted his rights to a monastery. Subinfeudation might mean that a knight's fee, a tenancy by which a lord was entitled to the services of one knight, was parcelled out by the tenant to three or four sub-tenants. Part of a knight is not an easy service to enforce. A knight's fee meant a knight's services for 40 days in the year. This arbitrary period, with no provision for training, was hardly suited to the needs of a professional army.

Therefore the 'mesne tenants', those who held from a lord other than the king, arranged with their lords that their military services be commuted to a money payment known as scutage, 'shield money'. The king's tenants, the tenants-in-chief, bought licences by which to avoid military service. By the fourteenth century, scutage was itself obsolete. By the fifteenth, services had no economic importance, though they retained for a time a social significance.

What has been said about military tenure holds also for serjeanty, which provided household and other services for the king, and to a lesser degree for other lords. The spiritual tenures of frankalmoign, where the religious services were uncertain, and divine service, where they were fixed, continued and are important to the legal historian. Their study is not, however, a necessary part of an introductory examination of the development of the common law.

INCIDENTS

Services lost their value and had little lasting impact on the development of the later law of property, but the incidents of tenure retained their worth longer, especially for the king, and left traces in the modern law. They represent a feudal reality, the claims that the lord could make because of the nature of the relation with his tenant. When the status of lord and man came to an end on the tenant's death, his heir no doubt had the feudal right to succeed. But the lord had rights, too, fixed by the feudal customary law which was law in the king's courts as well as the lord's courts until it was eventually replaced by the common law. The heir had to pay for the right to succeed. If the heir was an infant, the lord took the land back until the heir came of age. If the tenant died without an heir, the lord recovered the land for himself. Moreover, the customary responsibilities of a man to his lord included helping to ransom him and giving him presents on the great occasions when his eldest son was knighted and his eldest daughter married.

Although the lords lost most of these rights with the passing of feudal society, the king kept them for the income they produced which, because the king was lord of so many tenants, was great and regular.

ESCHEAT

If the tenant died without an heir, the lord recovered the land by 'escheat'. It was then his to keep or grant again as he wished.

RELIEF AND PRIMER SEISIN

If the tenant died leaving an heir, the lord exercised his right of 'primer seisin', that is he took back the land until the heir paid him a sum of money called a 'relief' and did homage, that is accepted the feudal status. During the period of his occupancy, the lord took the profits from the land. Magna Carta 1215 fixed the amounts that a lord could charge for socage land. A statute of 1267 abolished primer seisin, except for the king, who kept his rights against his own tenants.

WARDSHIP

If the tenant died leaving an heir who was an infant, the lord took the land back until the heir came of age. If the tenant had held the land by knight service the lord as guardian had the duty to bring up and educate the infant and, if he was male, to see to his military training so that he was fitted to assume the duties of military tenure and thereby to ensure his livelihood. In return the lord had the right to take for himself all the profits and, until Magna Carta stopped what had become an abuse, to waste the land, that is to exploit its capital of natural resources, for example by cutting its timber.

In a military tenure, the heir came of age at 21; in socage tenure, at 14; and the lord then had to account to him for the period of his wardship.

Wardships of military tenures were valuable investments in times when the laws against usury limited speculative opportunities, and they were widely traded.

MARRIAGE

When the lord became guardian of an infant ward, he took responsibility for his ward's marriage. There could be great profit in arranging marriages for wards or, bluntly, selling heirs and heiresses. The lord in theory could not force an unwanted marriage on his ward, for Christian marriage has always required consent, but by refusing an appropriate match the ward incurred the obligation to compensate the lord for his lost profit; and for marrying without the lord's consent the penalty was twice the value.

FORFEITURE

If a tenant was convicted of treason, his lands were forfeit to the king. The tenant's lord, if he was not the king, lost his rights too.

Forfeiture was the name originally restricted to that process but it also came to be used for the process of escheat which happened not as previously described on the death of a tenant without an heir but on the tenant's conviction of a felony (other than treason), because then the land fell forfeit to the lord.

AIDS

On certain special occasions the tenant had to make a contribution to his lord's specially onerous expenses. These occasions were fixed by Magna Carta as the ransom of the lord, the knighting of his eldest son and the marriage of his eldest daughter. The first soon became obsolete. A statute of 1275 fixed the amount for the latter two at 20 shillings for each knight's fee. Inflation took away their significance, except for the king's claims against his tenants-in-chief and even he could not raise 'aids' without the consent of the Council, the descendant of the *curia regis* and forerunner of Parliament.

FINES

What might well have become economically the most important incident was the fine which the lord could levy for his permission to allow the tenant to transfer his estate. When a tenant wanted to substitute a purchaser to take the tenant's place in the feudal relation with the lord, he needed the lord's agreement, which had to be bought. As alienation by substitution increased, fines might have been expected to become more important. But the statute *Quia Emptores* 1290, which prohibited subinfeudation (which avoided the fine), abolished fines at the same time as it required alienation to be by substitution rather than the creation of new feudal tenancies. But *Quia Emptores* did not bind the king, who continued to levy fines.

The king's income from incidents lasted for centuries. He had many tenants who had at some time to die. Some incidents befell them with satisfactory regularity: relief and primer seisin, escheat (and occasionally forfeiture), wardship and marriage, and, if they wanted to sell or otherwise dispose of the land, a fine was levied. It is not surprising that the legal advisers of the powerful tenants-in-chief found ways of avoiding incidents or that, when a king became powerful enough, he tried to stop them.

ESTATES

Feudal theory declared that all land was held directly or indirectly from the king. Tenure was the word which described the kind of services which the tenant owed to the lord.

Feudal tenure was based on status, the relation of lord and man, an arrangement by which land was granted in exchange for services. As this feudal relation became less important, a new status arose, the estate. As ideas of property developed, the feudal theory by which the lord held land from the king subject to the rights he had given to his tenant was supplanted by ideas of property in which the tenant owned land subject to feudal services and incidents which became less and less important. This ownership of the tenant was another kind of status, and called by that name in Latin. In English it was called an 'estate'. It too arose by arrangement between the original parties.

HERITABILITY

The original feudal grant was personal to lord and man and must therefore end on the death of either. The death of the lord soon ceased to affect the tenant's holding. Moreover, once the occupation of England was secure, the peaceful and efficient management of the economy became more important than personal military service. The lord was concerned to make sure that he got his revenue from services and incidents. His interests were served by giving the tenant what he wanted, the right to pass the tenancy to his heir. So he was happy to arrange the tenure in that way and make promises intended to benefit not only the tenant but his heirs. Before the Conquest land in England was heritable, usually by all sons equally. Soon afterwards it became heritable again, but with priority to the eldest son.

At first, a grant 'to Richard and his heirs' gave to Richard's heirs a personal right against the grantor. It was not at first a property right but, if the grantor refused to admit the heir in Richard's place, the heir from 1190 had a writ, the *praecipe quod recipiat homagium*, command that he receive homage, by which he could enforce his rights to inherit. To secure that special possession of the land called seisin, if the lord still refused to admit him, the heir had to bring an action of *mort d'ancestor* (death of an ancestor) to prove he was the rightful heir. In this way heritability was protected and enforced by law from the thirteenth century. The lord's ownership of the land thus became subject to a succession of life tenancies, until the heirs of Richard ran out. Neither Richard nor any of his heirs could claim more ownership than that.

THE FEE SIMPLE

The conceptual switch in ownership from lord to tenant came when a grant 'to Richard and his heirs' gave Richard the power to sell the land. It is at once obvious that heritability and alienability, the twin characteristics of landownership, are in conflict with each other. If a grant 'to Richard and his heirs' gives Richard the power to sell the land, the heirs may get nothing. On Richard's death his land would pass to his heir but Richard might in his lifetime sell the land and dissipate the proceeds of sale or will them away from the heir. As early as the thirteenth century, a grant 'to Richard and his heirs' gave Richard ownership and the heirs no right to stop Richard from alienating as he wished. Moreover, once Richard had sold to John, it was on the failure of John's heirs, not Richard's, that the land reverted to the grantor. The words 'and his heirs' created what came to be called a 'fee simple', as close to outright ownership as possible, bearing in mind that all land must be held of some lord and eventually of the king. They ceased to be 'words of purchase', giving something to those they named, and became 'words of limitation', describing the extent of the ownership, the estate of the grantee. Unless they were used, there could be no more than the primordial feudal grant, the life estate.

With the passing of *Quia Emptores* in 1290, subinfeudation was abolished and the lord lost the power to control his tenant's alienation and the fines that went to pay for the exercise of his discretion. With tenants in fee simple able to alienate as they wished, the last remnants of feudal reality had gone. The only link between tenant and lord was money. The switch was complete. The tenant was considered owner: the lord's rights an imposition on that ownership. As Milsom says:

The fee simple has become an estate, 'and his heirs' magic words to create it, and this estate, this ownership, has become an article of commerce. The feudal services are income, the incidents are capital gains, and land and lordship are being bought and sold for money.

The personal relation between lord and man no longer existed. The bond of status hardly survived. Instead there was property, land owned in all sorts of ways restricted only by the limits of ingenuity and the occasional intervention of statute or court. What had been seen by contemporaries as an attribute of status, and now seems to some observers to have been like the benefit of a promise, became an estate in land.

THE FEE TAIL

And so the lord's grant of land 'to Richard and his heirs' changed from a bundle of promises to a conveyance of property. But there had been other grants where the promise was more curtailed. The grantor might have wanted the grant to continue not so long as there was an heir to step into the shoes of the grantee but only so long as there was issue of the grantee or of the grantee and a named wife, perhaps the grantor's daughter. If the grant was 'to Richard and the heirs of his body' or 'to Richard and Matilda and the heirs of their bodies begotten' then the arrangement was that the lord undertook to admit in the former case only the descendants of Richard (and not his brother or niece), in the latter only descendants of the union of Richard and Matilda (and not a child of Richard's later marriage). This curtailed fee came to be known as an 'estate tail'. It would last as long as there were such descendants but then revert to the grantor or his heirs.

The rights of Richard's descendants to succeed to the fee tail would be defeated if Richard could sell. In the thirteenth century a fee tail was alienable — Richard could sell — once the first of the issue mentioned in the grant was born. The Statute of Westminster II 1285, Chapter 1, entitled *De Donis Conditionalibus* (on conditional gifts) was passed to stop this frustration of the intentions of grantors of fee tails. It provided that the form of the gift should be observed, and adapted the writ of formedon (*in forma doni*, according to the form of the gift) for the use both of a grantor whose intentions were frustrated and of the issue who were disinherited.

Freedom to alienate is, if unrestricted, a self-destructive licence. As uncontrolled freedom of enterprise leads to monopolies which destroy free enterprise, so unlimited freedom of the form of alienation would allow a grantor to tie up the land in a way which would prevent further alienation. There is conflict between the interests of the grantor, who wants to provide for his family (succumbing to the vanity of seeking to control the accidents of the future, including the risks of wastrel sons and improvident sales), and the economic interests of society, which demand that land shall not be tied up for long periods. This tension produced a remarkable system of interests in land of great complexity yet based on the two estates of feudal times, the fee simple and the life estate. The settlements which made use of those interests are described in Chapter 9.

REFERENCES AND FURTHER READING

Bloch, Marc, *Feudal Society* (Routledge and Kegan Paul, 2nd ed., 1962).
Brown, R.A., *Origins of English Feudalism* (George Allen and Unwin, 1973).
Critchley, J., *Feudalism* (George Allen and Unwin, 1978).
Macfarlane, Alan, *The Origins of English Individualism* (Blackwell, 1978).

8. The Rise of Equity and the Court of Chancery

THE CHANCELLOR

The common law courts grew out of the *curia regis* as its judicial work demanded treatment separate from other administrative tasks. The chief executive officer of the *curia regis* was the chancellor (*cancellarius*), who was the king's chief secretary and head of the royal secretariat, the chancery (*cancellaria*). The chancellor had two separate functions to perform in the legal process whose origins can be seen in Norman times: the issuing of writs and the hearing of petitions. From the start he and his clerks were of the clergy. He was not then a lawyer and his work was not considered judicial. Even now his successor's judicial functions are only one part of his many faceted job. The Lord Chancellor performs some of the tasks of a Minister of Justice, he is Speaker of the House of Lords and is invariably a politician of the government party.

As the king's chief secretary, the chancellor had custody of the great seal. It was he who applied it to the king's writs and all commissions of eyre or assize or oyer and terminer, whatever authority and instructions were given to justices, whether they were to deal with cases generally or only with those of a particular kind. He received petitions addressed to the king by those who wished the king to exercise his residual powers of judging the disputes of his subjects, when they believed his courts had failed or would fail to do justice. Many of those petitions the king or the petitioner would let the chancellor deal with himself. Then dealing with petitions became a part of the chancellor's job. The chancellor summoned the person against whom the complaint had been made to appear before him, by a letter called a *subpoena*, under the penalty of a fine and imprisonment in his gaol if he did not. By 1340 a court in Chancery is mentioned in a statute as having been in existence for some time.

In the thirteenth century, the chancellor sat as a judge not only in his own court but also with the common law judges from time to time, and they sometimes sat in Chancery. They were then all drawn from the same team. But as during the thirteenth century the common law courts had taken separate form and separate personnel, so during the fourteenth even their legal rules separated from those applied in the Chancery. The common law started to develop more elaborate but less flexible rules of law and procedure. Chancery's way of doing law jobs became a separate system, equity, which took much longer to become formal and has never become quite so inflexible.

It is essential to remember that the courts of equity were never Church courts. They always and totally belonged to the king. But from the beginning the chancellor was a cleric close to the king and as Milsom says:

> Although we have long ago ceased to look for the origin of that jurisdiction in some identification of the chancellor as the king's confessor, we shall also do wrong to assume that the whole truth lies in administrative details. The rise of equity is intelligible only if we remember the medieval familiarity with earthly institutions of conscience, and the medieval belief in an absolute right. Our own age is the first which has felt able to relegate the relationship between law and morals to the classroom.

PETITIONS TO THE CHANCELLOR

The chancellor's concern with petitions to the king from his subjects is already apparent at a time when it is still impossible to recognize common law courts separate from the king's administrative team, and when there were few rules of substance in our law, let alone a common law from which equity could be separate. While the law was undeveloped, a subject's idea of what was right, what justice required, was not. Though the king was not subject to his own courts, he too could infringe against that well-known justice and, if he did, his subject might ask him to redress the wrong. Whether the petition asked the king to put right a wrong which the king had done himself (or rather that an officer had done on his behalf) or that another subject had done to the petitioner, the king had responsibility for good government and, which might well be seen as the same thing, for justice in the realm.

Because it was usually necessary for those who sought redress for a wrong in the royal courts to start an action by writ, bought from the clerks of the Chancery, it was natural that, when for some reason they could not get a writ, they would petition the king, or in reality more likely the chancellor, for some other helpful intervention. The chancellor did not offer a body of law better or more comprehensive or more flexible or fairer than the common law. He did not always offer speedier or cheaper or more final justice, certainly not in later centuries. He did not offer to substitute for law a truer ethical system or a more refined reason. He was asked to do justice because there was some procedural or other artificial hindrance inhibiting the petitioner's use of the ordinary machinery of local or royal courts.

As the common law courts developed they applied a new national law, which came to be known as the common law, usurping the place of the different customary laws. That common law provided clear and simple rules concerned first with law and order, starting perhaps about 1166 with the assize of novel disseisin. By the time, in the first half of the fourteenth century, that a separate Chancery court can be discerned, there was a need for greater subtlety, particularly in questions of property. The chancellor's procedures had many advantages over those of the common law courts. They have been neatly described by Professor Baker:

The bill or petition required no formality, and the process which issued (the *subpoena*) was more advantageous by far than the common law *capias*. It enjoined the respondent to appear in Chancery and answer the petition under a fixed pain, often £100. For disobedience, the offender could be committed to the Fleet prison. No cause of action was stated in the *subpoena*, and so the petitioner was not tied to any form of action. The *subpoena* was not only completely general, it was ubiquitous; it ran into every county, even within liberties and franchises. The Chancellor had no jury, and could take evidence from the parties themselves. There were no rules of evidence such as those requiring deeds to prove debts and covenants. Evidence could be deposed locally before commissioners acting under writs of *dedimus potestatem* or upon affidavit, or by *viva voce* examination in Chancery. The court was not a fixed place, but followed the great seal and might convene in the Chancellor's private house. These differences were all procedural, but taken together the Chancery procedures were markedly less formal and in many instances more efficacious than those of the common law ... the litigant — aided by a learned profession — is ever astute to recognise that processes which are cheap, speedy and efficacious for one class of litigant, have attractions for all. The Chancery therefore came to be used by the landowning class in a large number of cases in which they might once have gone to other courts.

CHANCERY AS A SAFETY VALVE

In the sixteenth century rules of law as we now recognize them were forming out of the procedure of the common law courts. Chancery was seen by its supporters, among whom were still the judges of the common law courts, and by its customers, as a way of getting round the rigidity of a common law which could not be expected to provide a routine refined enough to do justice in all cases. When the result of a law suit was made to depend on the submission of a party's oath to divine judgment, by ordeal or even by battle, there could be no room for a disappointed party to petition for better justice elsewhere. But when ordeals were replaced by a fallible human decision then it was possible to think of a wrong decision and its amelioration. This equity provided, not by reversing the common law result but by leaving that decision where it lay and working on the conscience of the winner not to take advantage of the common law verdict. Much later, in the great case which fixed the superiority of equity over the common law, *The Earl of Oxford's Case* in 1615, Lord Ellesmere propounded the view of the function of equity then prevalent:

The cause why there is a Chancery is for that men's actions are so divers and infinite that it is impossible to make any general law which may aptly meet with every particular and not fail in some circumstances. The office of the Chancellor is to correct men's consciences for frauds, breaches of trust, wrong and oppressions of what nature so ever they be, and to soften and mollify the extremity of the law.

Common law courts henceforward could follow their own rules. The Chancery court would develop its own system, more concerned to act on the conscience of the person it held to be at fault. It would instruct, on pain of fine and in continued default imprisonment, the recalcitrant to perform the contract for breach of which common law would only award damages. It would enjoin the wilful to cease the behaviour which they had no right to continue but which the common law was powerless to prevent. It would make those who held property on trust carry out what they had been entrusted to do. The chancellor was usually a bishop and not a lawyer until Henry VIII appointed Sir Thomas More to succeed Cardinal Wolsey in 1529. It then became usual for chancellors to be lawyers and, after the ecclesiastical aberrations of Queen Mary I (1553–8), they were rarely clerics.

THE GROWTH OF EQUITY

A series of ingenious and scholarly legal technologists started at the end of the Stuart period with Lord Nottingham, 'the father of equity', in 1673 and ended a century and a half later with Lord Eldon. Throughout that period the chancellor himself said what equity was. At first he was the only judge in the court of Chancery. His later assistants, the Master of the Rolls and at the end of the period the vice-chancellor, were subject to appeals to him and he was effectively subject to very little supervision.

The great chancellors of that period took advantage of their power but did not impose upon those who petitioned them the vagaries of a capricious conscience. Burdened with the responsibility of discretion, they elaborated a body of law as complex though never as comprehensive as that of their common law rivals. The delays of Chancery became notorious. The problems caused by the duplicate jurisdictions ruined many a litigant. Yet in that period there were worked out not only the legal rules needed by the landowning families but, with the stimulus of jurisdiction given to the Chancery court by statute, many of the new systems of rules required by the burgeoning mercantile class. Throughout the second half of the eighteenth and the first of the nineteenth century, courts of equity provided most of the new rules of property law, of the conservation and disposition of wealth, which those who had power in society required.

Though equity was ancillary to the common law and could not have survived without the basic text upon which it was a gloss, so great is its vitality that more than a hundred years after the abolition in England of the Courts of Chancery in 1873, there is little sign of the body of law which we call equity dissolving in the common law. Indeed it still very occasionally produces new growth, where contemporary needs show the common law to be deficient and justice cannot wait for statute. It must be stressed that it does not often react to such a stimulus, and few judges are eager to encourage it. Every now and then even the highest courts will try to pretend that the Judicature Acts of 1873 were intended to fuse common law and equity into one undifferentiated body of law, which it is clear they were not from the parliamentary debates at the time. Failing that, judges may suggest that the amalgamation has happened since. That is equally obviously untrue. Certainly the courts of equity and common law and their procedures are no longer separate parts of the legal system. But the continued existence of the trust, with legal ownership in one person and equitable ownership in another, proves the separate existence of the two systems, to say nothing of interests and remedies recognized and available only in equity.

REFERENCES AND FURTHER READING

Maitland, F.W., *Equity* (Cambridge U.P., 2nd ed., 1936).
The Earl of Oxford's Case (1615) 1 Chancery Reports 1.

9. Succession and Settlements

SUCCESSION

When land was power, those who had the land were concerned to preserve that power for their families when they themselves could no longer exercise it. By 1250 the common law had fixed the rules of succession and forbade the transfer of land by will. The land must pass to the heir. Where those rules and that prohibition did not suit landowners, they and their legal advisers were astute in avoiding them.

At common law the rules of succession to land were simple and strict rather than fair or flexible. The rules governing succession to property other than land were quite different. In the thirteenth century jurisdiction over succession was shared. The common law courts dealt with real property except for manorial questions, including copyhold, which were the concern of the manorial courts. The ecclesiastical courts dealt with succession to personal property. The ecclesiastical courts encouraged wills, which were handy machinery for transferring property to the Church.

The canons or rules of descent of land were simply based on five principles: lineal descendants of the person last seised (that is, in legal possession) were preferred to collateral relatives; inheritances never ascended; issue took a dead person's place; males took before females of the same degree; sons took in the order of seniority, daughters in equal shares.

If the owner of land died leaving issue which survived, they took the land. Issue are children, grandchildren, great-grandchildren and so on. If not, the issue of the father of the deceased took. If there were none of these, then the issue of the grandfather, and so on. Therefore grandchildren of the deceased, for instance, had precedence over brothers of the deceased. An elder son took before a younger son; a son before daughters, even though they were older than him. Children of an elder son took before the younger son himself, even if they were daughters. An elder daughter took the same share as a younger. If the land came to the deceased from the father's side, collaterals on the father's side however remote took before collaterals on the mother's side. If the land came through the mother, vice versa.

For example, if Alan died, having had three sons, Bertram, Charles and David and two daughters Emily and Freda, and all his children survived him but the eldest son Bertram who died before Alan leaving no children but only three granddaughters Helen, Iris and Jane, daughters of his youngest daughter, Gertrude, then Helen, Iris and Jane would take all the land of their great-grandfather, to the exclusion of his surviving sons and daughters. The same would happen to the estate of a widow, Alice, as happened to that of Alan.

Although all legitimate issue were included, of whatever marriage, collaterals of the half-blood were excluded. Step-children still are. These old rules lasted until modern times. Some still beset the unknowing intestate (a person who leaves no will) and the unwary solicitor. They still govern such antiquities as hereditary titles and the royal family. Their continuance was possible because they could be evaded. The methods of evasion played a vital role in the development of the land law.

THE FEE TAIL (OR ENTAIL)

The problem which medieval landowners set their lawyers to solve was how to provide for their families in a more satisfactory way than did the rules of succession and other old common law devices, like 'dower', the ancient provision for a widow.

When rich people get old, they are tempted to try to hold on to the power they have been used to in life to control their families even after death. When they know they have not long to live, they are readier to loosen their purse strings, providing fine incentives to their lawyers to exercise their ingenuity.

Where great wealth was necessarily in land which could not be left by will, and the rules of intestate succession were arbitrary, the following problems needed to be solved.

The first problem was that the canons of descent gave all the land to the eldest son, giving nothing to the widow, younger sons, daughters or illegitimate children. That eldest son could sell and squander the proceeds, leaving his own family destitute. Landowners therefore were concerned in their lifetimes to make appropriate provision for all their dependants. They did this by granting pieces (or parcels) of land carved out of their holding to dependants who would not otherwise be provided for. They then settled the rest of their land; that is by a grant *inter vivos* (between living persons) they restricted the heir's rights to dispose of the land when he took it on the death of the present grantor.

It was usual on the marriage of a landowner for the husband to endow the wife with a parcel of land, to be hers on his death if she survived him. If no such grant were made, she would take at his death a reasonable part, at first depending on custom but which became fixed at one-third of his land. By 1350 a common law right to one-third of the husband's land (called dower) accrued to a wife on his death, irrespective of any grant.

There was no dower for the husband of an heiress. Instead the common law rule was that a husband who survived his wife held his wife's lands until his own death. This right, called curtesy, arose only once a child had been born of the marriage. The legal struggles were not, at least on the surface, between men and women but between men playing different roles, particularly the wife's father and husband.

The way in which the fullest ownership of land became the fee simple has been described in Chapter 7, where the fee tail was also explained. The fee tail was an estate limited to Arthur and the heirs of his body, which meant to Arthur for life and on his death to his issue — a child if one survived him, if not a grandchild. Usually the estate would be further limited, not only to the children of Arthur's marriage with Bertha, but also to his sons in order of seniority — all to the first, but if he died before Arthur without issue then to the second son and so on. If all the sons died before Arthur without issue, then to daughters in equal shares.

BARRING THE ENTAIL

The fee tail, sometimes called an entail, which was used to establish the family of a son or daughter, was subject to the risk that the tenant Arthur would manage to alienate (sell or grant away) the land. The statute *De Donis Conditionalibus* 1285 was clearly intended to make entailed land inalienable, but by 1400 there were ways of 'barring the entail', and transferring the land to a purchaser in fee simple. By 1600 this was done by a process called the 'common recovery'. This was a collusive action, based on fictions, by which Arthur, the tenant in tail, was able to transfer not only his limited interest but a full fee simple to a purchaser, Peter. This is how it was done. Peter brought a real action (the old formal claim to ownership of land) against Arthur on the basis of an imaginary title which Peter claimed. Arthur then got John to say that Arthur really had a fee simple (which was, of course, a lie because he had only a fee tail). This was called 'vouching John to warrant Arthur's title'. Arthur then failed to defend the action by Peter who got judgment by default. Peter became owner in fee simple, which was the object of the exercise. Arthur's issue were left with only an action against John for falsely warranting Arthur's fee simple title. But John was chosen because he was the court crier or some other person not worth suing. The remainderman or reversioner (the person who was intended to take if the estate tail failed) was similarly barred, dispossessed and left with the worthless action against John. John was a necessary element in the scheme because otherwise Peter would face an action in formedon on Arthur's death by the remainderman or reversioner or Arthur's issue. This scheme, of course, required the courts to collude in the fiction and turn a blind eye to the false swearing of John.

In the sixteenth century, donors tried to stop the barring of entails by providing in the grant that any attempt to alienate the land would for legal purposes be equivalent to the death of the tenant in tail, thereby ending his estate at once and accelerating the interest of the heir or remainderman. But in *Mary Portington's Case* in 1613 the court struck such a provision down as against the policy of the law which required that land should be alienable and that tenants in tail should be able to bar the entail. The collusive action was held to be effective and the collusion could not be pleaded. So much for parliamentary sovereignty in the sixteenth century! Those conservative common lawyers who fought against absolute monarchy were prepared to reform the law by striking down a statute of fundamental importance for the law of property on the ground that it was against contemporary public policy.

SETTLEMENTS

The urge of the landowner to look after his family according to his ideas of what would be best for them was satisfied by the settlement, which was made possible by the statute *De Donis Conditionalibus* 1285. That statute created the modern idea of the estate and thereby the settlement, because it allowed what would have been unthinkable in earlier feudal times, two fees in the same land, one in possession and one in the future, a statutory fee tail in the donee in possession, the fee simple remaining in the donor in reversion.

By 1300, an estate might be in possession, reversion or remainder. If Frank gave a life estate or fee tail to George, and Frank kept the fee simple, George had what was called a particular estate and Frank had a reversion. If Frank granted land to George for life, then to Henry and his heirs, George had a particular estate and Henry had the remainder. It followed that a remainder could not follow a fee simple. The reversion was itself a fee simple and was always vested, that is it belonged to an identified person, the grantor and his heirs. A remainder might be vested, but it might on the other hand be contingent. If the grant was to Mary (that is for life), remainder to Jane (that is for life), Jane was identified and the remainder was vested. But if the grant was to Mary, remainder to the heir of Jane, the remainder must be contingent, because at that stage no one could be sure who would become Jane's heir on Jane's death. It might look like Jane's eldest son, Claude, but Jane might outlive him so that Claude's son, or Jane's second son would then succeed.

The fee simple was freely alienable. The fee tail also had been made alienable by the stratagems just described. To tie the land up in a settlement meant giving no one either. The first feudal lords knew that no tenant had absolute ownership if one life estate was granted after another. But this could not be done by imposing limits on the estate. A grant 'to John and his heirs' had been held to give John a fee simple and nothing to the heirs. It was possible to give John a life estate and a remainder to Michael and his heirs. John could make no grant to extend beyond his death. Such a grant would require a resettlement on John's death. Moreover a grant to John for life, remainder to the heirs of John had for many years also been held to give John a fee simple. Therefore the settlement would usually try to do something like this: to John for life, remainder to John's eldest son in tail, remainder to John's younger sons successively in tail, remainder to Michael and his heirs. John's sons had contingent remainders. The fee simple was vested in Michael in remainder.

That kind of settlement posed many problems which were solved by a quite different device which had been known at least since the time of Domesday Book (1086): the use.

USES

It is essential to distinguish the technical term 'use' from the word in ordinary speech. Albert, owner of Blackacre, conveyed it to Richard, who became the legal owner in the ordinary way, except that Albert charged Richard with the duty of holding the land not for Richard's own benefit but for a purpose, to do a job, *ad opus* in Latin. In English that purpose came to be called a 'use'. By the thirteenth century uses were common. The duty undertaken by Richard might be an active one, perhaps to collect the rents and profits and pass them to Jane, but such active uses became uncommon. The normal use required Richard to do no more than play a passive role in a clever legal device.

Albert might convey Blackacre to Richard for the use of Jane, Richard was called the 'feoffee to uses', Jane the 'cestui que use', short for *cestui a que use le feoffment fuit fait*, 'the person to whose use the feoffment was made'. This device separated legal from beneficial ownership. The use had early been recognized by the common law to some extent and indeed it predates the separate systems of law and equity. But the legal ownership came to be protected by the common law, the beneficial by equity.

Many reasons have been given for the invention of this fruitful device. During the Crusades landowners went off for long periods to distant lands with no certainty of returning. The use was available to allow them to leave a trusted friend with the sort of powers, discretions and, they hoped, duties that would nowadays be given by a power of attorney to a lawyer. Franciscans took vows of poverty but wanted property. By the use they could have it both ways: all the beneficial ownership they liked without legal ownership. Presumably they considered that God was concerned only with that kind of property which was recognized by the common law. There were other less subtle kinds of dishonest purposes to which uses could be put, such as avoiding debts, and, as Christopher St Germain said in his book *Doctor and Student* (1518): 'It will be somewhat long and peradventure somewhat tedious to show all the causes particularly.'

By the fifteenth century, though no doubt uses were still used to defraud creditors, their main purpose was to allow the owner of land to leave it by will away from his heir, thereby making provision for other members of his family. While he was about it, he could take advantage of the use to avoid feudal incidents. Services were worthless but incidents such as wardship were still onerous. Common law did not now recognize uses, which could not be fitted into the scheme of estates. The cestuis que use had no estate. They had no seisin, the special possession recognized by the common law courts. They did not even have ordinary possession, which lessees had. Therefore common law would allow cestuis que use no writ: not a real action, which demanded seisin; not trespass (and therefore not ejectment) which required possession. Not even assumpsit was any good, because only damages could be recovered by it. Very occasionally a writ could be wangled, but that was hardly satisfactory. In 1402 the Commons had petitioned the king for a remedy against dishonest feoffees to uses, apparently with no result.

It was left to the chancellor to protect the beneficial interest of the cestui que use. His court, the Court of Chancery, and his law, equity, were described in Chapter 8. He did not attempt to disturb the legal ownership of the feoffee to uses. Rather he based his intervention upon it. He would summon Richard, the feoffee to uses, as legal owner of Blackacre, to account for his exercise of the responsibilities which it was alleged he had undertaken when the land was granted to him. The chancellor would place Richard on oath and interrogate him to find the scope of the use and whether his conduct had been unconscionable, then would make an order according to his findings. If Richard disobeyed the order, or had refused to submit to the questioning, he would be sent to prison.

By the second half of the fifteenth century, principles had emerged by which chancellors decided matters relating to uses, and by which they felt obliged to decide. There was a body of law and established routine procedures. Cestuis que use could therefore rely on a known standard of protection of their interest. This equitable interest, having the sanctions of the state to enforce it, had become thereby a new kind of property.

If Mary granted Blackacre to Richard to the use of David, then David became beneficial owner and Mary could not vary or detract from that ownership. If Mary wanted to grant Blackacre away from her heir James to her younger son, Jasper, then she might well do so by a grant to Richard to the use of Jasper in tail, remainder to James in fee simple. Only Richard had a legal estate, the interests of Jasper and James being equitable analogues of a legal fee tail and fee simple in remainder. And if Mary wanted to make a will of the equitable ownership of Blackacre, she would be able to do so by a grant to Richard to the use of herself, Mary. The equitable ownership of Blackacre did not pass on Mary's death to her heir but went wherever she willed it. By such a device Mary kept her discretion open until her death, because it would be the provisions as to succession to Blackacre found in Mary's will at her death which would prevail. Whereas a grant speaks from the time of its execution, a will speaks from the time of the testator's death.

An ancillary advantage of this device was avoidance of the feudal incidents that arose on the death of the legal owner. If Geoffrey took pains to grant Blackacre not just to Hugh, but, for instance, to a group of trusted friends or professional trustees, that is to lawyers, to hold jointly, there would be no opportunity for incidents to attach until the last survivor of them died. And if they had power to supplement their number as they dwindled, they could keep going and avoid incidents indefinitely.

The use had become so much a part of the scheme of property relations by the middle of the fifteenth century that uses were held to arise even where no express intention could be proved. Not only could Martin expressly grant Blackacre to Martha to the use of Martin himself, and thereby keep control of the beneficial ownership. If Martin granted Blackacre to Martha and Martha could not show that she had given good consideration for the grant, in other words she had not paid for it, then Martha was considered in equity to be a feoffee to unspecified uses to be announced by Martin, unless Martha could in some way show a contrary intention. This implied use was called a resulting use, because the beneficial ownership came back or resulted to Martin. Moreover, if Martin sold Blackacre to Martha but did not go through the formal routines of feoffment to complete the conveyance, Martha could not become legal owner. But in equity Martin held the land to the use of Martha. It would have been unconscionable for him to have done otherwise after taking her money.

Uses flourished through the fifteenth century and well into the sixteenth century but when Henry VIII felt sufficiently powerful and in need of money he sought to resume the feudal incidents of which uses had robbed him. First through his secretary Thomas Cromwell and the awful Audley, his chancellor after the death of More, and then directly and in person, he succeeded in persuading the judges to declare that while uses were not necessarily fraudulent, they could not be availed of to make a will of land which deprived the king of his incidents. Such a will was held to be void in *Re Lord Dacre of the South* (1535).

THE STATUTE OF USES 1535

In the same year was passed the Statute of Uses 1535, which by a simple trick robbed uses for a while of their value. It must have caused great consternation among lawyers at the time, particularly equity lawyers. The statute vested the legal estate in the cestui que use. The feoffee to uses was bypassed. A grant to John and his heirs to the use of Hugh and his heirs gave Hugh an immediate legal estate, a legal fee simple where before the statute his fee simple had been purely equitable. The use was said to be executed. The cestui que use had seisin; Henry VIII got his feudal incidents back; the common lawyers recovered much of their property work from equity; landowners, however, lost their power to make wills of their land.

By 1540 the king found it necessary to accommodate the demands of landowners to be able to leave land by will. The Statute of Wills 1540 was a compromise. The king's tenants in knight service were given testamentary power over two-thirds of that land. The other third passed to the heir and was subject to feudal incidents. Though wills of socage land were not restricted, if the land was held of the king the person to whom the land was left by will was for the purposes of incidents treated as the heir. Similarly over the two-thirds of land held of the king in knight service, which could be left away from the heir, the person who took under the will was liable to feudal incidents.

Since 1660, when military tenure was abolished, all land has been devisable by will.

One of the effects of the Statute of Uses, in executing the use, was to make a mere sale of land without feoffment (the formal public transfer) effective to pass the legal estate. As such a sale created an implied use in favour of the purchaser, he became legal owner by operation of the statute. But the whole point of the feoffment was publicity. It is important for the purchaser of land to be sure that the one who is purporting to sell has a good title and has not already sold to someone else. The Statute of Uses would have effected secret conveyances. As feoffment was so easily avoided, there was need for another technique to give public notice of transactions in land. The machinery was already in existence: registration. The Statute of Uses therefore contained a part, later called the Statute of Enrolments, which required all conveyances of freehold land to be registered by enrolment. But that statutory provision was neatly circumvented by a trick attributed to the cleverness of Serjeant Moore of the sixteenth century Court of Common Pleas: the lease and release.

The owner of Blackacre, Michael, who wished to sell it to Mary, would create a lease instead: Michael 'bargained and sold' Blackacre to Mary for the term of one year. There was no need of further formality to make Mary the lessee at common law because the Statute of Uses provided that the implied use which arose on the bargain and sale was statutorily executed and Mary became legal owner of the lease without further formality. Then Michael executed a deed of release of his rights as lessor to Mary, in other words, released to Mary the fee simple. The statute did not say that such a release had to be registered. That gave Mary a full freehold title secretly, by giving it to her in two parts, first the leasehold and then the reversion.

The Statute of Uses did little effective to avoid secret dealings and increased the complexity of conveyancing. It did not take long for conveyancers to find that all that was needed to get round the statute was to add eight more words to the conveyance to uses. If Hugh granted Blackacre to John and his heirs to the use of Kenneth and his heirs, the statute executed the use and Kenneth became at once the legal owner of the fee simple. To achieve his purpose, Hugh's lawyer would draft the conveyance 'to Leonard and his heirs, to the use of John and his heirs, to the use of Kenneth and his heirs'. The statute executed the first use and the words 'Leonard and his heirs to the use of' fell away, leaving the grantor's intentions intact. The word 'use' came to be kept for the one which the statute executed. The second use became known as the 'trust'.

THE STRICT SETTLEMENT

The settlement of land came to be organized by means of a wonderful piece of legal machinery which was modified and improved until it reached the refined efficiency of what was called the 'strict settlement', used in particular to set up a new family on marriage. The property was transferred to trustees to the following uses: to the new husband for life, subject to a 'rentcharge' (a perpetual annual sum charged on the property) to provide the wife with 'pin-money' (her personal allowance). The first remainder was to trustees, then to the first son, 'in tail male' (that is, and his male issue) then to the other sons in succession in tail male, subject to provisions for the life tenant's widow and other children, then to the daughters in tail, and finally remainder to the settlor.

That is a simplified description of the usual settlement. The reality was even more complicated, using leases to raise money for other dependants. When a son was born of the marriage, his remainder vested. When he was old enough he would be persuaded by his father to create a new settlement on the same lines, and so on for generations until modern times.

With the rise of capitalism, a further modification was needed. It was no longer the land itself that was considered all-important but the conservation and appropriate distribution of wealth. The tenant for life was therefore given the power to sell the land free of the fetters of the settlement, which fastened instead on the proceeds of the sale. The settlement has now been almost completely replaced by other schemes whose aim is more to avoid death duties and other taxes than to restrict the next generation's freedom of disposal. The urge to pass the tax burden on to someone else is now paramount but the basic tool of the inventive lawyer is still the trust, the use in modern dress.

REFERENCES AND FURTHER READING

Lord Dacre of the South's Case (1535). This case was reported for the first time in (1976) 93 *Selden Society* 228, the annual volume for 1976 of the Selden Society, which is devoted to the study and publication of material on English legal history. All its volumes are of interest and the serious student may well consider seeking membership from the secretary, Mr Victor Tunkel, Queen Mary College, University of London.

Mary Portington's Case (1613) 10 Coke's Reports 35.

Simpson A.W.B., *An Introduction to the History of the Land Law* (Oxford U.P., 1961).

St Germain, Christopher, *Doctor and Student* (1523 or 1528). There have been many editions. The most easily available is in Dr J L Barton's edition (1974) 91 *Selden Society*.

10. Trespasses and Torts

THE NATURE OF CIVIL WRONGS

There is no part of the law which so openly shows the social policy of a society, or rather of those who have power in it, than the law of torts or civil wrongs, that part of the law which deals with compensation for injuries to persons and their property. Social life inevitably leads to harm to individuals. In industrial societies the problems arise from road accidents and dangerous new machinery and newfangled products. In communal society the social disruption may come from cattle trespass or pigs straying into a neighbour's garden. The law of torts deals with the allocation of the burden of the damage which is caused, with who should suffer the loss and bear the risk.

Every society must provide two categories into which all such losses are divided. Into the first go losses which 'lie where they fall'. Those are the events which injure an individual but which the law does not concern itself with. There is no other person who must compensate the victim for the loss. Into the second go those losses which the law considers must be compensated by some person whom the law holds in some way responsible for the damage which has occurred.

Having decided that the burden should in some way be shifted from the sufferer to someone else seen as responsible for the loss, the law then has to decide what it is that has to be compensated for, what kind of compensation is to be paid and how much, and if there is any other kind of remedy which should be available.

The next chapter will describe the law relating to losses which arise from breach of contract. That is a kind of loss arising from another's conduct which is treated differently from other damage because it flows from a relationship between the injured and injurer which has arisen from an agreement between them. The contract itself has created the possibility of the damage. Where that damage is to fall and how it shall be compensated can also to some extent be left to the parties to decide. In the case of torts the relationship out of which the damage arises is less likely to be the result of the choice of those concerned. If you have agreed to sell me some raw materials for my factory and you do not deliver them on the date specified in the contract, then it may be that the contract itself will have something to say about how my loss should be paid for. If your car knocks me down in the street or if your pig strays into my garden and destroys my crops, there is no such agreement for me to turn to.

Chapter 4 described how the law of crimes grew out of the concern of the government with law and order. That concern was expressed in rules which laid down a tariff of compensation payments which were intended to take the place of tribal fighting or other forms of self-help. Wrongs committed by one private person on another were the concern of the king because they threatened the king's peace, but in addition to the fine payable to the king, the wite of the Anglo-Saxons or amercement of the Normans, there was compensation payable to the victim. That payment may look to modern eyes just like damages, whose intention is to make wrongdoers compensate victims of their wrongs, so that they shall bear the burden of a loss they have in some way caused and they, rather than the victims, are morally responsible to suffer, so far as money can help and so far as is reasonable. In the early law, though, compensation was not seen in that way. It was what was necessary to persuade injured parties not to take matters into their own hands, or to assuage the vengeance of their kin. The State intervened primarily because it had an interest in those matters being resolved peacefully and finally, and not continuing as a source of public disorder for generations of blood feuds.

TRESPASS

The machinery which the law offered to the injured party was based on the writ of trespass. The word 'trespass' is familiar to the modern reader in two contexts, represented by two well-known phrases. Signboards with the words 'Trespassers will be prosecuted' are used wherever English is the language of the law. Trespass is not usually a criminal offence, at least not on private land, and so the threat is often empty, but everyone knows what trespass means in that context — uninvited entrance on someone else's land. 'Forgive us our trespasses' is a part of the best known prayer in English. Nearly every child is taught to say it and some time later may understand what it means, simply 'wrongs'. The way to understand the writ of trespass and the growth of the law of torts is to forget the first meaning and to concentrate on the second. Although the law was at first most concerned with wrongs to land, to focus on that meaning is misleading. At first in the language of the law, the Latin *transgressio*, of which trespass is the English translation, meant nothing more specific than a wrongful act.

Looked at through modern eyes, the law after the Conquest distinguished great wrongs, which came to be called 'felonies', and lesser wrongs which were eventually called 'misdemeanours' if thought of as criminal and 'trespasses' if not. The writ of trespass gave instructions to the sheriff to summon the alleged wrongdoers to show why they had done the acts complained of. From its earliest form in the twelfth century it alleged that the defendant had injured the plaintiff *vi et armis et contra pacem regis* 'by force of arms and against the king's peace'. The wrong therefore concerned the king and that made it justiciable in the king's court. Otherwise it would have to be redressed if at all where by far the greater amount of such work was done, in the local courts according to customary law. The forceful wrong, breaking the king's peace, might be inflicted on the plaintiff's person, in which case the defendant was summoned to show why the defendant had insulted and beaten, wounded and ill-treated the plaintiff; or against the plaintiff's land, in which case the plaintiff had to show that the defendant had 'broken his (or her) close' or intruded upon the plaintiff's property; or against the plaintiff's goods by taking the plaintiff's goods and chattels and carrying them off. Whatever category the acts fell into, they were just the thing to start a feud, just the sort of behaviour which was most likely to lead to violent self-help.

Those who owned local courts were unwilling to lose jurisdiction over ordinary wrongs to the expanding grasp of the royal courts. They approved, therefore, of the royal courts' insistence that they would hear only those actions which involved an offence to the king. But the jurisdiction of local courts was itself limited by a rule which prohibited them from hearing actions where the value of the claim was greater than 40 shillings. That rule was enforced in some kinds of case certainly by the end of the thirteenth century, when 40 shillings was what a free labourer might expect to earn in a year if he was lucky. Inflation reduced the value of money gradually, and rapidly in times of plague and other scourges, so that 40 shillings ceased to be an appropriate amount by which to distinguish the large and important claims. But if local courts could hear only comparatively small claims and the king's courts only those where force was alleged, there was bound to be a great gap. What was to happen to claims above 40 shillings arising from non-violent wrongs? One answer was the fiction. Plaintiffs pretended that the wrong was violent when it clearly was not and hoped that the court would not allow any exception to be taken to the writ on that ground. The elegance of Fifoot's description cannot be improved upon:

When phrase becomes formula, fact declines into fiction. No sooner was the language of Trespass fixed than it was divorced from reality. In two cases in 1304 Chief Justice Bereford made the position clear. In the first the writ ran '*verberaverunt, vulneraverunt et ipsum ceperunt et imprisonaverunt*', (they beat, wounded and took and imprisoned him). The jury found that the defendants had indeed taken and imprisoned the plaintiff, but they had not beaten or wounded him. In the second, the plaintiff alleged that the defendants 'came tortiously *vi et armis* and cut and carried away his wood.' The jury found that they did cut the trees but not with force and arms. In each case Chief Justice Bereford disregarded the superfluous words as mere formalities and gave judgment for the plaintiff.

Thereafter it was accepted that though the formal words were still included, they could be there just 'to serve our writ' and the writ would be good though the evidence did not support them. Then towards the end of the fourteenth century writs began to be issued which omitted the allegation of force altogether.

TRESPASS ON THE CASE

The other answer was the creation of a new kind of writ and a new action, known as 'trespass on the case'. The writ of trespass had to include one of the three formulas set out on page 83; it had to show a violent attack on person, land or goods. The writ in an action in trespass on the case did not have to allege violence and did not have to fit those formulas. Instead it had to set out in detail what the wrong was, to show that the plaintiff had a 'special case'. That case was described in an additional clause beginning 'Whereas . . .' and setting out the facts.

The separate procedures in trespass and case were abolished by statute in 1504 but by that time the actions were quite distinct. There was great dispute, however, about what made the distinction. Some of the obscurity arose from faulty history. It was assumed that the action on the case was the creature of a statute of 1285, the

Statute of Westminster II, whose Chapter 24, entitled *in consimili casu*, 'in a similar case', gave the clerks in the Chancery the authority to create new writs by analogy with existing writs. The assumption that the action on the case arose from this source has only recently been considered of doubtful validity and the assumption was influential for centuries.

The more important source of confusion, however, was caused by another unhistorical urge, the need to find a conceptual rather than a procedural difference between trespass and case. The distinction was then drawn between direct and consequential injury. By the end of the eighteenth century it was possible for a judge to say that the distinction was perfectly clear: 'If the injury be committed by the immediate act complained of, the action must be trespass; if the injury be merely consequential upon that act, an action upon the case is the proper remedy.' The example often repeated was that if the defendant threw a log of wood into the street and hit the plaintiff the injury was direct and the action must be in trespass. If, however, the plaintiff's injury happened later, when she tripped over the log, the injury was consequential and the action must be in case.

NEGLIGENCE

By that time, however, the test was not apt to meet the demands of a rapidly changing society. The industrial revolution had filled England with new machinery and relationships between workers and masters and new kinds of products of novel technicality. In particular, new good roads produced vehicles which, though still horse-drawn, went much faster and caused many more road accidents. Railways some years later multiplied the opportunities for injury. Plaintiffs injured in road accidents at the end of the eighteenth century found themselves faced with a dilemma. If they could show that their injuries were caused directly by the defendant's act, they could sue in trespass. Trial judges told juries to find in the plaintiff's favour: 'If the injury was occasioned by the immediate act of the defendant, it was immaterial whether the act was wilful or accidental.' Yet other judges made a distinction where plaintiffs had themselves been at fault or their injuries were caused by 'inevitable accident'.

Nowadays liability would depend on proof of the defendant's negligence. It is not easy to show how the criterion of negligence, which gave birth to the modern tort of negligence, grew out of elements to be found in trespass and case, but it did. The forms of action were abolished by the Common Law Procedure Act 1852 and the modern law had not then been settled. Although the action on the case was the only one available to plaintiffs who had been injured by the inaction of the defendant or by some indirect cause, negligence was not a necessary element in it. Negligence is based on the principle that a duty of care was owed by the defendant to the plaintiff which the defendant did not perform. Such duties were known from medieval times. But then they arose from status. Those who carried on what were known as 'common callings', the innkeeper, the carrier, the surgeon or veterinarian, were liable to their customers for damage caused by their failure to do their jobs properly. Their inaction, called 'nonfeasance', or lack of proper care or skill, called 'malfeasance', were grounds for an action in trespass, and later in case. But the law had not yet developed a general duty of care.

Until the nineteenth century there was no general theory of liability for damage caused by wrongful acts. When plaintiffs, or rather their lawyers, were forced to base their claims not on a well-tried wrong such as trespass or one of the specific instances of case but upon a general contention that the defendant had a duty not to harm the plaintiff, the judges were faced with the policy choice with which this chapter started: is it right and wise to throw the burden of the loss caused by the defendant on to the defendant, or should it be left where it fell, on the plaintiff?

The judges of the nineteenth century, with no line of cases to fall back on, moved in fits and starts to cope with the demands made of them. If in one case a wide definition was given to negligence, as in *Heaven* v. *Pender* (1883), it was at once cut down by cautious judges afraid that too great a shift of the burden had been made. In that case the principle of actionable negligence was stated to be:

Whenever one person is by circumstances placed in such a position with regard to another that every one of ordinary sense who did think would at once recognize that if he did not use ordinary care and skill in his own conduct with regard to those circumstances, he would cause danger of injury to the person or property of the other, a duty arises to use ordinary care and skill to avoid such danger.

It was not until *Donoghue* v. *Stevenson* in 1932, however, that an eventually acceptable general description of negligence was propounded:

You must take reasonable care to avoid acts or omissions which you can reasonably foresee would be likely to injure your neighbour. Who, then, in law is my neighbour? The answer seems to be — persons who are so closely and directly affected by my act that I ought reasonably to have them in contemplation as being so affected when I am directing my mind to the acts or omissions which are called in question.

That such a vague and circuitous formula has been treated as hallowed for more than half a century shows just how intractable and unspecific is this very recent basis of tort liability called negligence. Because it depends on the social theories of the time, the allocation of loss arising from accident rather than deliberate wrong cannot be based on any more rigid rule. But, just because it is imprecise, the *Donoghue* v. *Stevenson* formula has served as a fruitful source of legal development.

The widening of tort liability put a greater burden on the rich, who owned the factories, railways, carriages and buildings by which the plaintiffs were injured. Poor men and women are not worth suing for damages because they have nothing with which to pay them. If they are injured, however, they sometimes have enough (or their trade union does) to hire a lawyer. It was the judges, of course, who expanded the scope of the law of torts. There were other judges, however, who preferred to restrict it. The majority were understandably concerned to protect the interests of their class. One of the greatest commercial judges of this century, Lord Justice Scrutton, himself well known as a conservative, had the insight to describe the phenomenon accurately in 1920:

[Impartiality] is rather difficult to attain in any system. I am not speaking of conscious impartiality, but the habits you are trained in, the people with whom you mix, lead to your having a certain class of ideas of such a nature that, when you have to deal with other ideas, you do not give as sound and accurate judgements as you would wish. This is one of the great difficulties at present with Labour. Labour says 'Where are your impartial judges? They all move in the same circle as the employers, and they are all educated and nursed in the same ideas as the employers. How can a labour man or a trade unionist get impartial justice?' It is very difficult sometimes to be sure that you have put yourself into a thoroughly impartial position between two disputants, one of your own class and one not of your class.

Two notorious tricks were used by judges not so introspective or determined to be fair. The first was called the 'fellow servant rule'. It said that if a worker was injured by the fault of a workmate, he or she had no action against their employer. The reason given was that the injured worker had willingly undertaken the risk of such injury. Of course it was a very unusual worker who could pick and choose among jobs until he or she was sure that all the other workers were incapable of negligence. There was in fact no reason for the rule, sometimes dignified with the name of the doctrine of common employment, other than the political one of judges protecting their own class.

Similarly, it was the judges of the nineteenth century who established the doctrine of contributory negligence, which denied an action to injured plaintiffs who could be shown to have been the slightest bit negligent themselves. A case in 1849 went so far as to hold that a passenger injured in a collision between two public carriages had no right of action at all against the driver of the other carriage who had caused the accident, if it could be shown that the driver of the carriage in which the injured person was travelling had also been negligent. The doctrine was preserved in full vigour against working people well in to the present century and abolished in England only in 1945, when power was given to the courts to apportion loss when both sides were partly at fault.

STRICT LIABILITY

In some circumstances the wrongdoer must compensate the injured person even if no negligence can be proved. Those who were held to be so strictly liable included keepers of dangerous things on their land, from fire and wild animals to water in reservoirs. No general principle was enunciated until 1867 in the case of *Rylands v. Fletcher*: 'Anyone who for his own purposes brings upon his land anything likely to do mischief if it escapes must keep it in at his peril.' Since that time the judges have been determined to cut down the scope of what they have seen as a dangerously wide principle. In the same way they have been careful to protect occupiers of land from claims by those who have entered and been injured by something on it.

Negligence was not the only modern tort to have its origins in case; and case, which grew out of trespass, quickly outgrew it.

There were other modern torts which had no connection with trespass which were developed by analogy through the medium of the action on the special case.

NUISANCE

There was an old real action of nuisance, which was only available to and against those who owned freehold land, for injury to it. The action on the case analogous to nuisance was available to anyone with any interest in land in possession against anyone who physically injured it.

MALICIOUS PROSECUTION

Malicious prosecution was created out of the old writ of conspiracy, which had itself been created by statute at the beginning of the thirteenth century. That writ was only available to a plaintiff who had been injured by two or more people maliciously conspiring to have him falsely charged with treason or felony. By the end of the fifteenth century the royal courts had approved an action on the case in the nature of conspiracy which was far wider. It could be brought where the false charge was made by one person only and alleged any kind of crime, whether felony or misdemeanour. That action became known as 'malicious prosecution'. Kindred torts were created by statute: 'maintenance', where a person sustained a legal action in which he or she had no genuine interest; and 'champerty', where such a person bought the right to share in the proceeds of the action. In some common law countries similar torts still exist, though maintenance and champerty have been abolished in England and elsewhere.

DEFAMATION

From early times a distinction was drawn between two kinds of defamation, statements which brought the person defamed into disrepute. The first was 'libel', where the words complained of were written or recorded in some other permanent form. The second was 'slander', for spoken words. Libel was the more serious wrong. It could give rise to a criminal prosecution as well as a civil claim for damages, even if no actual monetary loss could be proved. Like most other wrongs, slander was at first actionable in the local courts. Ecclesiastical courts also took an interest in the wrong done by evil speaking and would apply their sanctions to the wrongdoer. The royal courts gave an action in trespass to one who was insulted, because such an offence was a prolific cause of breaches of the king's peace. Actions for slander, on the other hand, based on the plaintiff's loss of reputation rather than likely violent response, were not known in the king's court until the middle of the sixteenth century. Then an action on the case for spoken words became available, from which the present action for slander was born.

The history of libel is quite separate from that of slander. It may well be that the wrong was not prevalent or important enough to warrant separate attention until the technology to perpetrate it became widely available. Printing made it both possible and dangerous. Criminal prosecutions were often brought in the Court of the Star Chamber, discussed in Chapter 12. That court came to give damages to the complainant as well as imposing criminal penalties. When the Star Chamber was abolished in 1641, actions on the case for libel began to be brought in the common law courts.

STATUTORY TORTS

Other torts were created by statute from time to time in response to social pressures and to combat recognized evils. After the undisputed power of employers over their servants (many of them serfs) was damaged by the shortage of labour following the great human disasters of the Black Death, an outbreak of the plague between 1348 and 1350, and the Peasants' Revolt in 1381, there were attempts to use the law to stop the natural shift in economic power from capital to labour. It became a crime to leave your employment (it was until recently in both Tasmania and Papua New Guinea and remains so for some occupations in Hong Kong) or to harbour servants who had left their jobs. An action on the case was fabricated for harbouring or seduction of a servant, which was later used generally in cases of seduction of women, with damages assessed upon the woman's value as a servant. The same Statute of Labourers 1349 which gave rise to those actions also produced the actions on the case for procuring a breach of contract and for conspiracy, which have been used since mainly in attempts by employers to contain the power of workers' organizations.

The law of torts continues to change rapidly and the common law world is now greatly fragmented in its legal responses to different perceptions of social needs. Insurance has become the great spreader of loss among the community as a whole or among those who gain advantage from the activity, such as motor car insurance. In New Zealand the whole community has taken responsibility for losses which individuals suffer as a result of all kinds of accident, at work, on the roads or even at home, and the State pays compensation based on the loss and has abolished the tort action which it has replaced. Other common law countries have partial schemes or still try to allocate risk and compensate for injury by using the old tools left over from the action on the case.

REFERENCES AND FURTHER READING

Donoghue v. *Stevenson* [1932] A.C. 562.
Fifoot, C.H.S., *History and Sources of the Common Law: Tort and Contract* (Stevens, 1949).
—— *Judge and Jurist in the Reign of Victoria* (Stevens, 1959).
Heaven v. *Pender* (1883) 11 Q.B.D. 503.
Manchester, A.H., *A Modern Legal History of England and Wales 1750–1950* (Butterworths, 1980).
Rylands v. *Fletcher* (1868) L.R. 3 H.L. 330.
Scrutton, Sir T.E., (1920) 1 *Cambridge Law Journal* 6.
Thorogood v. *Bryant* (1849) 8 C.B. 115.

11. Contract and Commerce

THE EARLY DEVELOPMENT OF CONTRACT

From primitive times people have made agreements which they have intended to bind them, promises which were solemn, but it has not always followed that the community would enforce them. Charondas in Ancient Sicily is said to have expressly provided in his laws that promises should not be enforced:

All buying and selling is to be for cash and the law is to provide no remedy for those who lose their money by giving credit.

And Plato two centuries or so later, in Classical Athens, wrote in chapter XI of his *Laws*:

Our next need will, of course, be a proper regulation of our business transactions . . . In all reciprocal exchange by means of sale and purchase, goods exchanged are to be delivered on the sites appointed in the market square for the various articles and the price is to be received at the time, exchange is not to be permitted in any other locality, and there shall be neither selling nor buying on credit. If any citizen makes any exchange because he trusts the other party, he must do so on the understanding that the law allows no action.

It was shown in Chapter 3 that in Anglo-Saxon England there were formalities for cattle sales which were strictly enforced and whose neglect might be prima facie evidence of theft. With the growth of commerce and the nation state comes the realization that enforcement of a promise is not just a matter of the promisor's standing with the gods or reputation in the community but for the sanctions of the state.

Because contract arises from agreement between the parties, the first problem is proof. What evidence is there that there was any agreement, as the plaintiff says? The first sources of our contract law come from a time when the technology of writing was not readily available. Even now it is not practicable to demand that there be written evidence of all contracts. There were written contracts in Anglo-Saxon times, used for grants of land and even wills. But the common law early made the distinction not between written and oral contracts but between formal contracts and informal contracts, whether written or oral. The former were called 'specialties' or 'deeds', the latter 'parol contracts'.

COVENANT

Commercial contracts were enforced in the merchants' courts of borough or fair or port. The Church courts concerned themselves with breaches of faith. The local courts handled most of the business we should now classify as arising from contract. They had their different methods of proof and their own customary law. But by the fourteenth century the common law courts would accept only one form of proof of an agreement, a deed. The common law did not discriminate about the contents, type or purpose of the agreement. All 'covenants' were enforceable but covenant had come to mean an agreement incorporated in a deed. The royal courts enforced covenants: other contracts were enforced by other courts, if at all. This looks now like a technicality without substantial justification but there was a reasonable and practical distinction. If the transaction was weighty, it should have been done by a deed: if not, why trouble the royal courts?

DEBT

The royal courts, however, did deal in other ways with conflicts which we would consider as arising out of contracts. The writ of debt was available in the Court of Common Pleas to recover money (or other things) owed by defendant to plaintiff. There had to be a fixed amount. The action was not given for the defendants' broken promises but arose from the defendants' obligation to give back what was not theirs. If Mary sued John for a specific chattel which she said was hers but John was wrongly detaining, the writ was called detinue. If instead it was for what Mary alleged John owed her, it was debt. The obligation did not have to arise from an agreement at all. That was not the question. The problem of proof was solved either by a deed or, in its absence, by showing that Mary had given a *quid pro quo*, 'tit for tat'. It was not generally enough that she could show that she had merely made a promise. She had to show that she had performed her part already. Moreover,

Common Pleas allowed John to wage his law, to bring oath-helpers to swear that he was honest and worthy of belief when he said he owed Mary nothing. Hardly a satisfactory process for creditors to rely on.

The writ of debt was available not only to recover a fixed sum arising from a loan or the unpaid price of goods. Other kinds of performance could be enforced by creating a bond, which was a deed by which a promise was made to repay a loan on a certain day (or perform some other obligation) and in default to pay a certain sum of money. To make sure that, for example, John performed the services as he had promised her, Mary would make him undertake by deed to pay a fixed penalty if he did not perform his promise adequately and in time. On breach, Mary sued in debt on the bond for the amount of the penalty. She had the deed as proof of the obligation. It was easy to prove that the time for performance had passed. John had to pay unless he could prove that he had been formally discharged, which he could usually do only by showing that Mary had given him back his bond.

The conditional bond was in general use even into the nineteenth century. It had many advantages for the creditor, many drawbacks for the debtor, whom equity progressively protected against fraud and some other kinds of unfairness.

TRESPASS

It has been shown in Chapter 10 how the writ of trespass took many forms as it grew in scope and importance. The king's courts came to accept jurisdiction over a widening range of wrongs. England was a prosperous commercial nation with much trade of all kinds both internal and international. The government took an interest in all matters of trade, from which it raised revenue and some of which it controlled in detail by statute. In the fourteenth century, the law had a special concern for what became known as the common callings. Those who carried on certain crafts or trades were subject to control: innkeepers, carriers, smiths, veterinarians for example. If they did their job badly, with less care and skill than was usual in their trade, the injured customer could bring an action against them in trespass.

Nowadays we make a sharp distinction between a contractual obligation, which arises from the parties' own voluntary assumption of responsibility, and liability in tort, which does not arise from promise but from a breach of duty imposed by the state irrespective of the parties' wills. But a motor mechanic, who negligently repairs a car, may be liable both for breach of contract and in the tort of negligence. In the fourteenth century, a smith who negligently shod a horse so that it went lame committed a trespass. It might even then be thought of also as a broken undertaking to do a proper job and if no such undertaking had been expressly given it might be implied from the smith's practising a common calling. If an action on the case lay for such a breach, why should it not lie for the breach of any undertaking? A broken promise is a wrong, after all, and damage, injury, flows from it.

To deny the action to some suitors was a matter of policy. The comfortable 'floodgates' argument is time-honoured among judges as among all decision-makers. Bluntly it is: 'Let us not do justice in this case, lest tomorrow we be overwhelmed by the flood of plaintiffs who will ask for justice too.' The royal courts in the fourteenth century decided that they would grant no remedy in trespass unless the defendant had actively done a wrong. Omitting to do what was promised did not count. The negligent smith had actively driven the nail into the quick, a 'malfeasance'. The smith who promised to shoe a horse but did not was guilty of mere 'nonfeasance', for which no action of trespass would lie. The king's courts knew where to draw the line. They would enforce a covenant, a solemn formal document as the seal showed. They punished breaches of the king's peace by actions of trespass. But, though they winked at other shams, they would not allow mere nonfeasance to be dressed up as trespass. Yet at the same time, the need was growing for the development of a general principle of contract liability.

DECEIT

One factor which contributed to this development was the action of deceit which lay against those who caused damage by fraud. In the fifteenth century, the judges came to accept that, if Mary could show that she had paid for John's performance and he had broken his promise to perform, she had an action in deceit and it did not matter that the wrong complained of was nonfeasance. Deceit would lie even though on the facts the plaintiff could have sued in debt.

ASSUMPSIT

Through the sixteenth century there were cases which took the development of contract law a little further, but in fits and starts. There could be no general principles apt for the new needs of commerce and industry until the policy was accepted that mutual promises made a contract and would be enforced by the State. That was the new shape that the problem of liability for nonfeasance had assumed. The action of debt required plaintiffs to show that they had already performed at least part of their side of the bargain; the action from which the modern law of contract grew, though it was like debt in some ways, had no such requirement. It allowed plaintiffs to sue on the broken promises of defendants, even if they had performed nothing themselves, that is even if the contract were wholly executory, nothing having been done on either side other than the giving of promises. This new action was 'assumpsit', which means 'he has promised'. It developed in the second half of the sixteenth century and flowered in a case at the start of the seventeenth. It was consciously fostered in the King's Bench, from that court's stock of trespass techniques, to compete with the monopoly which Common Pleas had over debt.

In *Slade's Case* in 1602 Slade brought an action in the King's Bench to recover the price of grain from the purchaser. The action was in the form called *indebitatus assumpsit*, 'having become indebted, he promised'. The jury found that the purchaser had bought the grain but had made no express promise to pay separate from and after the deal. The purchaser did not want to face an action in assumpsit, with a jury weighing the evidence. He would have preferred to be sued in debt, where he could wage his law. In those days there were no law reform commissions. Parliament did not consider it its duty to develop the private law.

A sensible but unusual method was adopted of taking what was at the time recognized to be a momentous decision. All the judges of the royal courts met together to hear the policy and the law thoroughly argued. This extraordinary court held that every contract made by mutual promises could be sued on in *indebitatus assumpsit*: 'every contract executory imports in itself an assumpsit.' The question 'can you sue even though you cannot prove a separate later promise to pay?' was given an answer containing the subsequently all-important rule that mutual promises made a binding contract, enforceable by the modern action of assumpsit.

The test of a binding contract came to be consideration — the price for the promise. Reciprocal promises were good consideration one for the other. Consideration was defined twofold: in terms of some detriment to the promisee (the injury required by all trespass actions and their derivatives) or benefit to the promisor (the performance by the plaintiff which the action of debt had required). But the essence of contract was bargain.

FREEDOM OF CONTRACT

Freedom of contract, or licence to exploit economic power, is a part of the political philosophy of liberalism or laissez-faire, itself a product of an economic system which had grown to rely on 'the market forces' or 'free exchange' rather than custom, tradition or authority for the distribution of resources.

Land and labour had become commodities to be freely bought and sold by the end of the Middle Ages. The growth of capitalism in the eighteenth and nineteenth centuries saw an increasing division of labour and a concomitant increase of productivity. There had to be an efficient market through which raw materials and finished goods, money and labour could smoothly flow. There had to be contracts which allocated risks and profits and the State had to realize how important it was to enforce them. As Adam Smith wrote:

> The foundation of contract is the reasonable expectation which the person who promises raises in the person to whom he binds himself; of which the performance may be extorted by force.

The basis of contractual liability in the common law is economic self-interest. But in the right hands even base motives may be sanctified:

> If there is one thing more than another which public policy requires, it is that men of full age and competent understanding shall have the utmost liberty of contracting, and that their contracts when entered into freely and voluntarily shall be held sacred and shall be enforced by courts of justice.

Judges like Sir George Jessel, who used those words in 1875 in *Printing and Numerical Registering Co.* v. *Sampson*, manufactured much of the modern law of contract on the basis of their social and economic philosophy. That law prevails still in many countries and has to be assessed in the light of present needs. The most intractable of individualists must recognize the need for change, for it is in the preservation of the rights of the individual that the common law has failed. Something has been achieved. The control of those exercising the common callings has been shown to be as old as the common law itself. Old statutes subject moneylenders to the scrutiny of the courts. In this century there has been a growing recognition of the need for the State to control monopolies and restrictive trade practices. There is in most common law countries much new law to protect the consumer and borrower. The question is no longer whether freedom of contract is sacred but how far the State should intervene to ensure that freedom of contract is not used by groups, powerful economically or otherwise, against rights of an individual which in a civilized society ought to be protected.

REFERENCES AND FURTHER READING

Atiyah, P.S., *The Rise and Fall of Freedom of Contract* (Clarendon P., 1979).
Hughes Parry, Sir D., *The Sanctity of Contracts in English Law* (Stevens, 1958).
Plato, *Laws* translated by Benjamiw Jowett (various editions).
Printing and Numerical Registering Co. v. *Sampson* (1875) 19 L.R. Equity 462.
Simpson, A.W.B., *A History of the Common Law of Contract: The Rise of the Action of Assumpsit* (Clarendon P., 1975).
Slade's Case (1602) 4 Coke's Reports 91a.
Smith, Adam, *The Wealth of Nations* (many editions).
Stoljar, S.J., *A History of Contract at Common Law* (Australian National U.P., 1975).
Excellent short accounts are Appendix I of Allan, D.E. and Hiscock, M.E., *Law of Contract in Australia* (CCH Australia, 1987) and Chapter 1 (by Simpson, A.W.B.) in Furmston, M.P., *Cheshire, Fifoot and Furmston's Law of Contract* (ELBS 11th ed., 1987)

12. Fictions and Jurisdictions

CHAPTER 5 told the story of the common law courts until the fifteenth century, by which time they were clearly divided into King's Bench, Common Pleas and Exchequer. Chapter 8 described the rise of equity and the Chancery court. This chapter is concerned with the development of the courts until they took their modern form at the end of the nineteenth century.

COMPETITION FOR JURISDICTION

For two centuries the three royal common law courts appear to have vied with one another for jurisdiction but it would be wrong to attribute that competition to greed for fees. A much more likely and continuing impetus to expand the jurisdiction of each court came from the attempts of lawyers to find new procedures quicker, cheaper and more likely to win them the result their clients wanted.

By 1500, the Court of Common Pleas had jurisdiction over nearly all ordinary work of the royal courts. It heard pleas between one subject and another, begun by writ from the Chancery, and had exclusive jurisdiction in the real actions and older personal actions of debt, detinue, account and covenant. It supervised the work of local and manorial courts. It shared with King's Bench actions in maintenance, conspiracy and other breaches of statute as well as actions in trespass and case and their offspring, including ejectment. Its advantages in being stationary, having a body of highly skilled advocates with special status, called serjeants, and its monopoly of the real and older personal actions gave it the bulk of business throughout the Middle Ages.

During the sixteenth century, however, Common Pleas lost its lead. The older forms of real action had been largely made obsolete by the action of ejectment (described in Chapter 6). The personal actions were supplanted by others derived like ejectment from trespass or case. Both King's Bench and Exchequer perfected fictions to provide better and often cheaper service to litigants.

THE BILL OF MIDDLESEX

The first trick devised by lawyers practising in the King's Bench was to persuade the court to extend artificially the jurisdiction which it had in any kind of case over those who were already before it (and therefore technically its prisoners) in another case. A party before the court in one action within the court's genuine jurisdiction, such as in trespass, might be sued while there, for debt, which would otherwise be outside it. The plaintiff also saved the cost of a writ to get the defendant before the court. The opportunity to get at defendants in the King's Bench in this way was not restricted to the plaintiffs who had brought them before the court in the first place. They were fair game for anyone who found them there.

The King's Bench judges extended their jurisdiction by going a step further. They created the fiction that a defendant who was not before the court at all had committed a trespass within its jurisdiction. The court no longer followed the king around. It settled at Westminster in the county of Middlesex. It could allow an action without a writ for a wrong committed within that county. The action could be started simply by letter, by a bill. If the wrong arose in any other county, a writ from the Chancery would be necessary, which had the double disadvantage of being costly and also subject to independent scrutiny of the Chancery clerks who would direct the plaintiff to the Common Pleas. So the King's Bench invented an elaborate subterfuge, called *latitat*. The Sheriff of Middlesex received a letter from the court, the Bill of Middlesex, which alleged that the defendant had committed a wrong within the county. The defendant was not, of course, within the county or the procedure would not have been necessary. The sheriff, therefore, made a return on the bill of *non est inventus*, 'he has not been found'. The court then issued a process to the sheriff saying that the defendant *latitat et discurrit*, 'lurks and runs around', instructing the sheriff to find and bring the defendant before the court. The fiction was so normal by the 1540s that there was no need to bother with a Bill of Middlesex. The plaintiff started the action with the *latitat*.

AC ETIAM

By these means King's Bench took business from Common Pleas and writ fees from the Chancery. A patent of 1608 allowed the

Chancery clerks a fine of half the writ fee for every *latitat* issued for debt. In 1661 a statute required the true cause of action to be stated, not the fictitious trespass. King's Bench got round these attempts to restrict its jurisdiction by allowing the plaintiff to keep the old procedure and merely add to the fictitious trespass a clause beginning *ac etiam* 'and also' which set out the genuine cause of action.

Common Pleas retaliated with its own form of the *ac etiam* device but by that time there was plenty of work for both courts to do and their rivalry became unimportant for their future development. King's Bench retained its precedence because of its supervision of the work of other courts, including the Common Pleas. The local courts over which Common Pleas had had control fell into disuse.

QUOMINUS

Competition for jurisdiction was not restricted to the major courts. The Exchequer of Pleas had been restricted since the thirteenth century to the collection of money owed to the king. The speed and efficiency of this small court's work attracted the notice of the legal advisers of those with debts to collect and they were able, with the connivance of the 'Barons of the Exchequer', as its judges were always called, to bring their actions to recover debts there.

If John owed money to the king and pleaded that the reason he could not pay was that he was owed money himself, the Exchequer of Pleas would lend John its aid to recover against his own debtors. If those debtors in turn said that they could pay only when they recovered from their debtors, why should not the court see the whole thing through, as far as necessary? From such splendid logic are fictions born. If John comes to the court and seeks its aid to recover his debt, pleading that the amount he is owed makes him so much less able to pay his debts to the king, why not hear him, without enquiry into the reality of those royal credits? The writ of *quominus* recited that John by so much less was able to pay the king. The court did not enquire whether John's debt to the king was really as much as he was now claiming. Soon they did not concern themselves whether it existed at all. Not only actions for debts but also claims for damages could thus be brought in the Exchequer of Pleas. By the end of the sixteenth century, it shared with its two greater partners the jurisdiction over actions for debts and damages.

From the end of the sixteenth century ordinary civil actions were heard in all three courts. King's Bench also dealt exclusively with the great criminal trials, constitutional matters, and errors alleged against the other courts; Common Pleas had some relatively unimportant exclusive jurisdiction; and Exchequer still dealt with cases concerning the royal revenues. The division and the overlap continued until the reforms of the nineteenth century. The local courts lost all their jurisdiction to the courts of the central government and customary law was eventually supplanted by that central government's law, the common law, though not completely in matters of land until 1925.

CHANCERY

Yet the resurgence of the common law courts did not give them undisputed ascendancy. *The Earl of Oxford's Case* in 1615, described in Chapter 8, and James I's statute of the following year, gave precedence to the Court of Chancery and to its body of law known as equity.

Every student of history or law or politics is familiar with the struggle between conservative and modern ideologies in Henry VIII's time (1509–47) and later, in seventeenth century England, personified by Chief Justice Coke and James I, between common lawyers in parliament and the ambitions of kings to set up an absolute monarchy with the aid, if necessary, of an alternative system of justice through novel courts. The Court of Chancery, represented in that drama by Francis Bacon, the Lord Chancellor, was not the only possible substitute. There was a new profession of civil lawyers, trained in Roman law at Oxford or at Cambridge by a new professor specially created for the purpose by Henry VIII, rather than with the common lawyers in the old Inns of Court, where legal education had been monopolized for centuries.

THE COUNCIL

The Chancery court was not the only court outside the common law system which was created from the king's closest advisers. The king's council, the *curia regis,* gave birth not only to the king's common law courts and the Court of Chancery; from it sprang the forerunners of parliament, which has a long and fascinating history too large to be treated in a sketch of the common law, and also of the Privy Council, for centuries the highest equity court and until modern times an important court of appeal.

The Council had started as the henchmen of William the Conqueror, had been transformed over the centuries first to a group of squabbling aristocrats whose rivalries threatened the kingdom, then had become in the time of Edward IV (1461–83) and Henry VII (1485–1509) a team of 50 professional administrators, drawn from the bishops, judges, canon lawyers and common lawyers of the highest rank. Through a large part of the long reign of Elizabeth I (1558–1603), a smaller group of the heads of government departments, including the Lord Chief Justice, the Comptroller of the Royal Household, the queen's secretaries, the Treasurer of the Chamber and the Chancellor of the Exchequer, were overwhelmed by petitions which they tried to send to the ordinary courts and eventually refused to receive unless they concerned 'the preservation of her Majesty's peace or shall be of some public consequence.'

THE STAR CHAMBER

The Council was particularly concerned with treasons, as political opposition was called in those days, and got itself commissioned to examine those suspected of crimes against the State, whom it was in the habit of imprisoning for long periods without trial. When the Council met as a court rather than by special commission, and heard cases pleaded before it, that court came to be known as the Star Chamber, from the name of the place where it sat. It was at first another equity court, doing much the same kind of business as the Court of Chancery, under the presidency of the Chancellor. But the Star Chamber took a special interest in cases which touched the government of the king, particularly threats to law and order. It had a reputation for tyranny and certainly terrified those it brought before it.

With the other conciliar courts, the courts which stemmed from the king's council, it was abolished in 1641 at the start of the reforms of the Long Parliament which eventually led to the revolutionary Commonwealth and the temporary overthrow of the monarchy. The jurisdiction of the Privy Council was restricted to hearing appeals from outside the scope of the ordinary courts of law and equity: from certain disciplinary bodies, from some admiralty and ecclesiastical courts, from the Channel Islands and from the Plantations, as the colonies were then called. Its appeal jurisdiction, exercised by its Judicial Committee, became of great importance during the heyday of the British Empire but now has almost disappeared.

NINETEENTH-CENTURY REFORMS

Throughout the nineteenth century the system of courts was reformed in bits and pieces until by the Judicature Acts of 1873 the old courts were swept away and a new High Court of Judicature created, whose divisions, though they carried the names of the old Courts of Common Pleas, King's Bench and Chancery, had general jurisdiction in common law and equity. Another division, variously labelled over the years, dealt with miscellaneous matters such as had previously been handled by ecclesiastical courts and courts of admiralty.

By that time the British Empire was at its zenith. The common law had been transported (sometimes with convicts) to all parts of the world. The attempts to plant common law on alien soil have been extraordinarily successful, though whether it grows as a source of sustenance or as a noxious weed can be argued about by future generations. In some countries, such as Australia, it is the only source of law. In others, like Papua New Guinea, it has been explicitly adopted by the constitution on independence, alongside communal customary law. It will be guaranteed in Hong Kong by the Government of the People's Republic of China. However it is assessed, the common law is a most remarkable achievement of the English.

REFERENCES AND FURTHER READING

Cornish, W. R. and Clark, G. de N., *Law and Society in England 1750–1950* (Sweet and Maxwell, 1989).
Manchester, A. H., *A Modern Legal History of England and Wales 1750–1950* (Butterworths, 1980).

13. The Languages of the Common Law

THE LANGUAGE AT THE NORMAN CONQUEST

It would be natural to assume that, from the time of the Conquest, William I and his Norman successors would have insisted that their dialects of French should be the language of administration and particularly of law. What else could they use?

French did become one of the languages of the common law, but when? The ancestors of William the Conqueror (on his father's side, the word 'bastard' being introduced to England first as his epithet) were Danes. King Charles the Simple of France acknowledged Rollo as Duke of Normandy in AD 912, after they had been there about a century. They may have been speaking some kind of French by then. There is an old tale that the second duke had to send his son away to school to learn his forefathers' language.

Two things must be kept in mind. First, only the English would have considered the Normans really French. Secondly, there was nowhere before the twelfth century any one language which could be called French. There were many dialects in what we now call France. If they were written down, then 'French would become Latin if you tried to write it at its best', as Maitland saw.

Ethelred the Unready had married the Duke of Normandy's daughter in 1002 and their son Edward the Confessor spoke French like his parents, and his court included Normans and seemed very French to the English. Edward told William, Duke of Normandy, that he had chosen him to succeed — or so William said. He was only a second cousin but that was closer than Harold Godwinson, who had sworn, under pressure, to support William's claim. Of course William was illegitimate and could have no claim of blood at all. So he took England by force and ruled as a military dictator.

But what effect did the Conquest have on the language of the law? Latin replaced English. William may have kept on Regenbald, who had been Chancellor to Edward and possibly to Harold, perhaps with a secretariat we might anachronistically call the Chancery.

Yet, though for a few years some writs and taxation records were in an archaic Old English, Latin soon became the main language of official documents and records, and the only one after 1154.

It was the Church that most consistently and influentially introduced French and developed it in England. Just as William replaced the defeated English landowners with his own men, mostly Norman speakers, so he also substituted French-speaking clergy for English. The Church controlled all education. The Church taught Latin in French; only after the plague in 1348 did schoolboys construe their Latin in English.

In the first century after the Conquest, Stubbs says, 'French was the language of the court, Latin the language of the Church and English the language of the people.' The truth is more complex. Many clergy spoke French and not all the French-speaking Normans were at court. Moreover, French had an advantage as a fairly standard lingua franca over any of the widely-differing dialects of English. Southern Standard English was a long way off.

French literature in England begins with a translation from Latin, done for Henry I's queen Adeliza in 1120, of the *Voyage of St Brendan* by a monk, Benedeis l'Apostile. It ends in the fourteenth century with Gower, the trilingual writer. But by that time there was a strange language, unknown to all but the lawyers and a few others, which became known as Law French.

THE CHRONOLOGY OF LAW FRENCH

French was the language of legislation only from 1266 to 1483, and then not exclusively, but it was the language of the courts for some purposes from the Conquest to the eighteenth century. William I and William II did not speak English. Any courts they attended must have used the kind of French which was the only language the kings and many of their great officials understood. Similarly the monolingual Normans who presided over other courts could not work in English. Henry I may have known some English but he would hardly have relied on that knowledge in dealing with legal matters. Henry II understood but did not speak English, it seems. However much the Norman kings insisted that they were reinstating the old pre-Conquest English law, they had to do it in French, if they or their closest allies were personally involved.

Lawyers as a profession are conservative. They rarely initiate reform when it is not in their interest. The rest of England might stop speaking or writing French, as later it stopped wearing wigs, but lawyers continued to work in what became Law French, as contrived a survival as the barrister's wig. Once lawyers had started to take notes in French they would not change their language as what they recorded gradually changed from mainly French to mainly English. Those for whom they were recording did not change their needs either and were happy to be members of the same small language fraternity.

No one knows when or how Law French developed. There is much fascinating work to be done by scholars who are thrice qualified, as historians, lawyers and linguists, and as trilingual as the lawyers and others needed to be from the Conquest on. The problem is that the evidence is, of necessity, written. The task of describing the development of the written languages is comparatively easy. What is hard is working out the role and the progress of the spoken language. When did Law French become one of the languages of the common law courts and when did it cease to be? What purposes did it serve? Did the note-takers write what they heard?

It is easy to show the earliest document in English, Latin or Law French and also the latest, though new discoveries are likely to push the termini further apart. It is not easy, however, to show when a language was first spoken and when it fell into disuse.

OFFICIAL RECORDS

The language in which legal documents were written changed after the Conquest from a form of Anglo-Saxon, probably too archaic to be widely understood, to Latin, the only language in which one could be adjudged literate. Throughout the Middle Ages '*litteratus*' meant having the ability to read Latin. Writing was not essential, that being a craft rather than an intellectual accomplishment, and some could write who could not read. The art and craft of writing was distinct from the art and skill of dictating, taught in the universities.

French was spoken not only at the royal court; it was the speech of the nobility, or at least those who kept close connections with France, and it was the language of management. It was undoubtedly used in the royal courts of law, but it is not clear to what extent.

The evidence is extensive but it must be kept in mind that it is, of necessity, written. No other record of language was possible until the invention of the gramophone. Writers will occasionally tell us what was spoken but their words are rarely unambiguous.

THE WRITTEN EVIDENCE

Immediately after the Conquest, the written language of administration was undoubtedly Latin. One scholar who examined the 487 writs and charters surviving from the first two Norman kings (1066–1100) puts the score as follows:

Old English: 19
Both Old English and Latin: 9
Latin: 459
Any kind of French: 0

Richard FitzNigel wrote in 1179 an account of the workings of the Exchequer, where he was Henry II's Treasurer, in Latin in the form of a dialogue between Scholar and Master. Master is made to say:

But nowadays, when English and Normans live close together and marry and give in marriage to each other, the nations are so mixed that it can scarcely be decided (I mean in the case of freemen), who is of English birth and who of Norman.

Could they not be distinguished by their speech? If not, all freemen must have spoken English. They can hardly all have been speaking some kind of French.

The Year Books are given an important place in Chapter 14. Depending upon their definition, the first known Year Book to have survived is the report in Latin of the London Eyre of 1244. From the start of Edward I's reign (1272) they are in French. Is that evidence that the language used by the court was Latin or French? The first distinction to be drawn is between different parts of the hearing. It would not be surprising if evidence were taken in the vernacular, usually English but sometimes French. The legal argument was regularly in French. The same sort of thing, I know from personal experience of observation of bilingual practice, happens now in Papua New Guinea and Hong Kong. What probably happened in the king's court was that the parties and the witnesses were addressed by court and counsel in English when that was their language but that court and counsel argued and deliberated in French, though that changed over 500 years until the only remnants of what had become Law French were in the formal narration of the pleadings in those cases where such a recital was necessary, and in the oral judgment.

There is no doubt that about 1285 the pleadings were read out loud in French: '*per narratores in romanis verbis et non in latinis pronunciantur*', as a thirteenth century law book says, 'pronounced by pleaders in French words and not in Latin'. Was testimony taken in French? Maitland seems to have thought it was. The early Year Books are full of dialogue that is fresh with the tang of original speech, not only between lawyers but with witnesses. Yet no more fresh than the manuals we know to be fiction.

Church courts in the thirteenth century used Latin but testimony could sometimes be given in English and an appeal might be explained in both French and English.

In the fourteenth century an integral part of an action at common law was the count, the plaintiff's detailed story. It was carefully recited in French by a professional counter or narrator. In 1310, one of the Templar defendants is noted as giving evidence in English, so one may guess that the others did so in French.

English was first used in Parliament in 1337.

THE FIRST LEGISLATIVE ATTACK

In 1362 England was at war with France. The great English victories at Crécy (1346) and Poitiers (1356) had been won and Calais recaptured. Patriotic feeling among the great majority whose mother tongue was English, and even among the few of the nobility who still spoke French, may have produced an aversion from the language of the enemy. The publication of Langland's *Piers Plowman* (1362) showed that English was a language fit for decent and serious literary use. Chaucer would soon start on the *Canterbury Tales* and Wyclif on the *Gospels*.

Whatever the background, Parliament passed a statute in 1362 which banned the use of French 'much unknown in the said Realm' and required the use of English in all proceedings in all courts.

The Statute of Pleading was in Law French, as all statutes were, if they were not in Latin, until 1483. It is not ambiguous. Having recited the disadvantages of French it forbids its use: 'all pleas which shall be pleaded in any courts whatsoever, shall be pleaded, shewed, defended, answered, debated and judged in the English tongue' though they will continue to be 'entered and enrolled in Latin'. Not only the arguments in court — *'debatuz'* it says in the statute — but the written pleadings and the judgments must henceforth be in English. It says nothing about oral evidence, perhaps because that had for a long time been taken in English only.

What happened? Historians of any period learn not to assume that behaviour changes to conform with new legislation. Children did not disappear from mines or factories in nineteenth century England or bonded maids from Hong Kong homes in the twentieth because legislation required them to do so. Official supervision of the implementation of safety legislation is at best intermittent and avoidance may be expected. But the courts were public, in Westminster Hall, under the noses of king and parliament. Yet the king's own highest courts disobeyed, to some degree and at least for a time, the statute's clear provisions. Maitland wrote, 'We know that it was tardily obeyed, and indeed it attempted the impossible.' Fortescue wrote just over a hundred years after the statute that although the statute had restricted the use of French 'as much as possible, it had not managed to get rid of it altogether.'

Though English thereafter was probably used invariably for taking evidence and possibly for almost all other parts of the trial of an action, there is evidence that Law French continued as the language of oral pleadings, where they were still used. Archbishop Cranmer said — and he must have been writing of a time between 1510 and 1549 — that he had heard suitors complain 'because their attornies have pleaded their cases in the French tongue.'

Modern reports start in 1571 with Plowden, Dyer (1585) and Coke (1600). The Year Books survive until about 1622. The language of them all was French. The first professional legal text in English comes from about 1450. Fortescue wrote in Latin but was translated into English in 1567. The second volume of *Doctor and Student* had been written in English in 1530 but for its political propaganda rather than its law, and it was the only law book in English as far as Coke was concerned.

Coke and his contemporaries preferred French. They openly expressed their fears of the mischiefs made possible by law in a language ordinary people could understand — as did some of their contemporaries about the Bible. As Coke said 'lest the unlearned by bare reading without right understanding might suck out errors, and trusting to their conceit, might endamage themselves.'

THE SECOND LEGISLATIVE ATTACK

By 1649 it is clear that both evidence and argument were in English. Maitland believed French 'might sometimes be heard in the courts of law, more especially if some belated real action made its way thither. The pleadings ... were also put into French in order that they might be "mumbled" by a serjeant to the judges, who, however, were not bound to listen to his mumblings, since they could see what was written in "the paper books."' These mumblings are reported as late as 1739. Written pleadings continued to be in Law French.

But in 1649 there was revolution. Charles I was executed and the monarchy fell. The new rulers of England had no time for medieval nonsense or the tools of old privilege. 'In 1650 and 1651, Parliament, complying with a petition from the army and with the general wish, enacted English should be the language of the law.'

There were lawyers who supported the revolutionary changes, like Brownlow, who in 1652 was happy to write works in English to replace what he termed 'those vast and unwealdy Volumes, ... rendered useless, by ... their obscurity, being writ in an unknown Tongue.' But there were also others who complained and bided their time. In 1660, the monarchy was restored. The legislation of the Commonwealth was abrogated. Reports and statutes were once again published in French. And Charles II was French where he was not Scots.

THE FINAL LEGISLATIVE BLOW

Law French lived on for 70 years after the Restoration but at last in 1733 and 1735 two statutes compelled the lawyers 'to use their mother tongue'. The judges were as usual against reform. Lord Chief Justice Ellenborough said it would make attorneys illiterate. Lord Raymond said the law would have to be translated into Welsh. The 1733 Act required that:

All proceedings whatsoever in any courts of justice within that part of Great Britain called England, and in the court of exchequer in Scotland, and which concern the law and administration of justice, shall be in the English tongue and language only, and not in Latin or French, or any other tongue or language whatsoever.

ENGLISH LAW IN ENGLISH ONLY

This time there was no rearguard action, though plenty of reactionary regret. And there were still fine lawyers who preferred to write in French, and perhaps to think in it. The conservative Roger North championed the Law French in which his brother Francis, Lord Keeper, wrote his notes until his death in 1685. He even went so far as to say, two years after the 1733 Act, 'For really the Law is scarcely expressible properly in English, and, when it is done, it must be Françoise, or very uncouth.' And he insisted even then that still, in court, 'Counts, Bars, and such transactions as reach no farther than the Bench and Counsel, with the Officers, and not to the Country [i.e. to the Jury] . . . are to be done in Law French.' He must have been describing the oral use of Law French, at its last muttering gasp.

What sort of a language was Law French when it died? It had started out as the language of the elite, 'the normal tongue of the educated classes after the Conquest, the Oxford accent of the day', as Fifoot said. By the eighteenth century it was easy for an English law student to pick up — 'so very easy to be learned, that the meanest wit that ever came to the study of the law doth come to understand it almost perfectly in ten days without a reader.' Or so an Irish judge thought. So, how foreign was it?

THE ASSIMILATION OF FRENCH AND ENGLISH

The English language at the time of the Conquest had already been affected by influences from France. Of course, both languages are Indo-European and spring from the same stock, linguistic historians agree. From 1066 to 1466, more than a thousand 'Romanic' words were imported. Nearly twenty had arrived by 1154, including important legal terms: 'justice', 'peace' (in its legal sense), 'prison', 'privilege', 'rent' and 'robbery', as well as 'court', in no specifically legal sense. All those words are found in one work, the *Peterborough Chronicle*. By 1200 or thereabouts, in the *Ancren Riwle*, written in verse and a southern dialect, are found more than four hundred such words, so assimilated that they could be given English prefixes and suffixes, as in 'bi-spused', espoused. Maitland gives a remarkable list of law words taken into English from the French, claiming that, 'It would hardly be too much to say that at the present day almost all our words that have a definite legal import are in a certain sense French words.'

Pronunciation was anglicized and was little affected by the changes that had taken place in France. In the moots which students performed in the Inns of Court, from medieval until modern times, fines were imposed on those who affected the pronunciation of France. No Frenchman could comprehend the Law French of the eighteenth century. The contemporary historian Taine described it: 'no doubt a colonial French, damaged, pronounced through closed teeth, with a contorsion of the throat, not in the style of Paris but of Stratford-atte-Bowe.'

Now what all this means is clear. There was no sharp transition from Law French to English, from one distinct language to another. What legislation insisted on first in 1362, again in 1650 and finally in 1733, had been going on gradually all the time. The structure and syntax of French and English are similar. When spoken for generations bilingually, they tend to be assimilated. By the seventeenth century certainly the spoken vocabulary of monolingual English law students, if there had been any, and the written vocabulary of Law French were becoming one, because English by that time had adopted a Law French vocabulary. Though it seemed to the law reporter Burrows in 1766 that there was a clear distinction between 'a fixed dead language', protected from vulgar corruption by its strangeness, and the 'fluctuating living one' it was not by then possible to 'withdraw its vocabulary from popular contact', as Maitland said. It had, to all intents and purposes, become a dialect of English as much as of French. As Blackstone wrote:

And yet in reality ... as the English and Norman languages were concurrently used by our ancestors for several centuries together, the two idioms have naturally assimilated, and mutually borrowed from each other: for which reason the grammatical construction of each is so very much the same.

The 1733 Act was more important in abolishing the use as a language of record of the other language of English law: Latin.

LATIN

Baker puts it neatly: 'Lawyers wrote notes in French and kept records in Latin.' That has been true of Latin for nearly six hundred of the eight hundred years of the common law's life. From when they begin (1100) to the time of Henry VII, statutes are in Latin (or sometimes French or both). Henry VII's are in English but, from Henry VIII they revert to Latin. From their origins to modern times, lawyers needed a good grasp of Latin. Manners, routines, techniques and skills may change in court, and with them language, but 'the custom of an office or a department upon a matter of second-rate importance, such as the language used in making up a record, is perhaps the most conservative thing on earth,' wrote Holdsworth.

With French, Latin came back at the Restoration (1660). But by then those who wrote Latin were forced by changing circumstances, the poverty of their skills and the need to make accurate sense to their readers to incorporate English words.

TENTATIVE CONCLUSIONS

If the Year Books were, at least from about 1450, verbatim notes taken in a language other than that in which the words were spoken, two conclusions may be drawn. First, those who took them were bilingual enough to be able to produce reports of the quality and comprehensiveness that we have. But there was nothing new in that. Lawyers had had to be trilingual for centuries. Magna Carta was ordered to be read in every shire. Those who were to read it received a Latin or a French copy and must have been intended to read it out, perhaps having prepared themselves, in whatever dialect they expected their audience to understand. Secondly, it is not surprising that the Year Books are not more polished. Even the cleverest and quickest could hardly be expected to produce prize prose compositions. Why did they cling to that procedure? Because it was a good jargon in which to think about the common law and the users for whom they wrote — themselves or those who bought their notes — thought in the same jargon. They would not worry too much about solecisms of grammar. They would not find it amusing if the writer, being too rushed to think of a French word, stuck in an English one. In a Latin record, written in less of a rush, he would have to excuse himself with an '*anglice*' (in English) or '*vocatus*' (called) — for example '*pixides pro necotiano, anglice tobacco jars*'. In a law report he could unselfconsciously write: '*4 Curtens et Vallens serra intend tam que est use circa un Bed.*' 'Four curtains and a valence will be meant, such as is used around a bed.' 'Circa un Bed' — Latin, French and English — would have brought any schoolboy a beating, but it was good enough shorthand for a lawyer to understand.

REFERENCES AND FURTHER READING

Baker J.H., *Manual of Law French* (Scholar P., 2nd ed., 1989).
Baugh A.C. and Cable T.A., *A History of the English Language* (Routledge and Kegan Paul, 3rd ed., 1978).
Blackstone, Sir William, *Commentaries on the Laws of England* (many editions).
Clanchy M.T., *from Memory to Written Record* (Edward Arnold, 1979).
Fitz Nigel, Richard, *Dialogus de Scaccario: The Course of the Exchequer*, Charles Johnson ed. and translator (Clarendon P., 1983).
Mellinkoff David, *The Language of the Law* (Little, Brown, 1963).
Pollock F. and Maitland F.W., *The History of English Law before the Time of Edward I* (Cambridge U.P., 2nd ed. (2 vols.), 1898, reprinted 1968).

14. The Literature of the Common Law

THE common law is a written law which displaced the largely oral customary laws; a national law which supplanted the limited jurisdictions of Saxon kingdoms, of counties, of feudal manors, of mercantile ports and boroughs and fairs, of special franchises and royal prerogatives and eventually even of the Church. Some of those jurisdictions had their literatures but even canon law cannot match in richness the unequalled literature of the common law.

The sources of the common law are to be found in legislation, reports of decisions of the courts and books written for lawyers. Legislation has the greatest authority, though it was not always unchallenged. Reports of cases not only chronicle the development but provide authoritative statements of the law. Other books are not now treated as authority though some have been in the past and are still given great respect.

LEGISLATION

It may seem strange to include legislation within literature at all. Certainly some of the least attractive prose is to be found in the statute books but not only is 'literature' meant here to include any written source of law, there is also much legislation which, at least after age has mellowed it, becomes of literary as well as legal interest. 'Legislation' is the generic word used for all kinds of enacted laws, whatever their source of authority. The word 'statute' is a synonym for an act of parliament and best not applied to enactments before there was a recognizable parliament or legislation of colonial legislatures or other bodies with delegated powers.

The English constitution has never been based upon any careful separation of powers or functions into legislative, judicial and executive. As Winfield wrote of the first 200 years after the Conquest:

> The country had to be governed, and, so long as the rules necessary for it were made, no one inquired very closely how they were made or who made them, and no one thought it remarkable that laws were often framed by judges, and that law cases were often heard by the legislature.

Law laid down by any organ of the central government was the king's law. It was enough that it had his approval and there was no means of questioning it. A law might have different names in English, just as there were different words in French or Latin, the other languages of the law. We have encountered 'assize' used for legislation made at Northampton and Clarendon. Just before them there were the Constitutions of Clarendon. Later there were the Provisions of Oxford. The word 'statute' did not become usual until the time of Edward I (1272–1307).

Moreover, the form of legislation was not settled early. Depending on its origin, legislation might look like a grant by the king, a proclamation of victorious rebels, an agreement between rival political factions or even a writ. The present requirement of the approval of parliament dates from the beginning of the fifteenth century. Until then, legislation was, like a judgment of his court, an expression of the king's will. There are private collections, which are necessarily incomplete, from the thirteenth century. From the end of that century official rolls started to be kept, though they did not become complete and reliable until 1483 and the commencement of the Inrollments of Acts of Parliament, which continue in much the same form to the present day not only in the United Kingdom but elsewhere where similar parliamentary systems prevail.

At about the same time, printing of law books began in England and a collection of statutes from 1327 onwards appeared, called the 'New Statutes', *Nova Statuta* in Latin. The 'Old Statutes', *Vetera Statuta*, from the earliest to 1327, were published in 1508. Later there were abridgments of all the statutes, or at least those the printer could get copies of, and from 1557, with William Rastell's *Collection in English of the Statutes from the Beginning of Magna Charta unto 1557*, there began the private publication of attempts at a complete collection of all the statutes in force to date, usually with some such title as *Magna Charta cum Statutis*. Ruffhead published his *Statutes at Large* (that is, not abridged) from 1762, perhaps the most popular collection, going through many editions, until an official version was published by the Record Commission (1810) of legislation up to 1713. An official series *Public General Statutes* has been published since 1831. Today, most lawyers use one of the commercial series: *Halsbury's Statutes* or *Current Law Statutes*, which are annotated.

LAW REPORTS

Unlike most other legal systems, English law has another source in addition to that which flows from the legislature. Indeed, even though statutes are most authoritative, their authority derives from the common law and their meaning is authoritatively stated by the common law. That common law is to be found in the words of the judges published in law reports.

The earliest reports are the Year Books. They are more or less verbatim reports of the arguments of counsel and the court and of the judgments themselves, in cases in Common Pleas, in eyre and much later in King's Bench. They run for nearly four hundred years, from the mid-thirteenth to the mid-seventeenth century. They were at first published in manuscript copies and called 'term books' because they were collected and sold a legal term at a time. When they came to be printed, they were collected by the year, each volume containing a number of years, and were known as Year Books. There is controversy about who made them and who used them but it is likely that they were aids to learning and remembering the law the judges declared, particularly the rules of pleading, the special technology of the new profession of barristers. No one has yet discovered how the Year Books were distributed before printing. It seems as if until about 1450 there was one original note-taker at a time, whose manuscript was copied, perhaps commercially. After 1450 there was more than one original. The emphasis became less upon pleading and more on what we should now call substantive law.

The Year Books began to be printed about 1500. By 1600 the printers had collected and published those up to 1535. The standard printed collections are inaccurate and incomplete but, because they were cheaper, they replaced the better sources, the manuscripts, which were discarded.

Once there was more than one original text of reports of the same case, they had to be distinguished, so they were given the names of the reporters. There are manuscripts of reports as late as 1622 which are just like earlier Year Books. However, 'nominate reports', those known by the reporters' names, were published from 1571 (Plowden) and 1585 (Dyer). Coke's great series began in 1600. The nominate reports were first published, like Year Books, in manuscript form. When they came to be printed, from about 1650 on, poor manuscripts were often used and little trouble was taken to name the reporters accurately. Indeed, reports with well-known names attached sold well, particularly those of famous judges and, if they were dead, the publishers could with impunity pass off the work of inferior scribes.

It was only towards the end of the eighteenth century that law reports were published regularly and not long after the decisions they reported. By then they covered Common Pleas and King's Bench, Chancery and a little later Exchequer.

A great collection of these nominate reports, the *English Reports*, was published in 1932. Although by no means complete, it is the first resource for lawyers seeking reports of cases before 1865, when the Council of Law Reporting started to publish the semi-official *Law Reports*. Today there are many series. Every common law jurisdiction has some form of reporting. In the United States of America and the United Kingdom there are all kinds of specialist series. The general reports best known in England are those which appear weekly, the *Weekly Law Reports* and the *All England Reports*. In some smaller jurisdictions the official reports are expensive and intermittent but there are usually less formally produced reports, known quaintly as 'unreported judgments'.

TEXTBOOKS AND OTHERS

It is hard for a law student lost in the luxuriant jungle of a modern law library to believe that even as late as 1800 a lawyer would need to study only a hundred or so titles to be truly learned in the law. Nearly all of them were written expressly to help in that study and nearly all of the best were by judges.

Learning the law was at first a matter of listening and remembering what went on in the Court of Common Pleas. The Year Books helped. To make them more useful the books needed an index. More efficient still was an abstract of the points of practical use, alphabetically arranged. Lawyers and students made such abridgments for themselves and some were published. The first, called later *Statham*, was published in 1490, then *Fitzherbert* (1516) and *Brooke* (1573). Not only did they make it easier to find authorities in the Year Books, they included references to cases in manuscripts not otherwise available.

The abridgments grew into digests — attempts to state all the law in encyclopaedic form, the greatest of which were *Viner*

(1741–53), *Comyns* (1760) and *Matthew Bacon* (1763–6). The modern encyclopaedia of English law is *Halsbury's Encyclopedia of the Laws of England*, now in its fourth edition, with commentaries attempting to keep it relevant in some other jurisdictions. *The Digest*, formerly the *English and Empire Digest*, is closer to the traditional digest of cases.

The lawyer's craft required other handbooks. 'No remedy without a writ', though a half-truth, illustrates the need for learning about writs. Lawyers kept their own precedents, then as now, up-to-date and annotated. But beginners need an introduction and busy lawyers fall behind with their reading and need reassurance that they have not missed or forgotten something. One of the earliest printers, Winkin de Worde, published *Returna Brevium*, 'Returns to Writs', in 1519, William Rastell *Registrum Omnium Brevium*, 'A Register of All Writs', in 1531. Lawyers also needed precedents of pleadings, first the formal counts or *narrationes*. They were supplied by *Novae Narrationes*, first in manuscript and then printed before 1500. The counts were oral and in French. When written pleadings in Latin were needed, 'books of entries' were published, the first in 1510.

Lawyers still use precedents — of pleading like *Bullen and Leake*; of court forms, *Atkin*; and of all kinds of legal documents, not necessarily connected with litigation, the *Encyclopedia of Forms and Precedents*, and are likely to continue to need them even though they now store on their own computers the forms they use most often.

The kind of law book most familiar to students is the textbook, ranging from the monograph on one topic to the attempt to cover the whole of the law. Such books have an 800-year history in England, as long as that of the common law itself. The earliest is *Tractatus de Legibus et Consuetudinibus Angliae*, 'A Treatise on the Laws and Customs of England', written about 1189, reputedly by Ranulph de Glanvill, Chief Justiciar of England and Henry II's first choice not only as judge but as general and right hand man. It deals with the procedures of the royal courts and was printed first in 1554. A much more ambitious book with the same title was written about sixty years later and published under the name of Henry de Bracton, a judge of the King's Bench from about 1248 to 1257. Bracton's notebook on which he based his book has survived. It shows his method of extracting his law from the current plea rolls. It is a magnificent early piece of judicial scholarship, written in Latin.

Students preferred their books in French and *Britton*, written about 1290, supplied the want of an easily accessible text, partly following Bracton. Later texts, the *Old Tenures*, an introduction to the land law, and *Natura Brevium*, which introduced the study of the writs, were added to the stock of manuscript texts a hundred years later. A century later, Littleton, a judge of the Court of Common Pleas, wrote the *New Tenures*, a better and, of course, more current primer of the law of real property. In the sixteenth century there were attempts to bring the practice books up to date and the appearance of a new kind of book altogether, St Germain's *Doctor and Student* (1528). This was in the form of a dialogue between a student of the common law and a layman — doctor of divinity — and is an attempt to explain and justify the common law in terms of morality.

We have met Coke in these pages before. Not admirable in many ways, as a man, a lawyer or a scholar, he was nevertheless the most influential writer the common law has ever had. He wrote, in four parts, *Institutes of the Laws of England*. The first part, the greatest, was published in 1628 as a commentary on Littleton's land law. Baker's insight is splendid: 'He wrote like a helpful old wizard, anxious to pass on all his secrets before he died, but not quite sure where to begin or end.' His digressions, full of false etymologies and credulous history, make the dull stuff of the land law fascinating.

A much better scholar and writer, though without wicked old Coke's charm, is Matthew Hale, whose posthumous publications, *History of the Common Law* (1713) and *History of the Pleas of the Crown* (1736) set new standards, not only of literary style but of clarity of structure and presentation.

The book which marks the beginning of the modern era of legal textbooks is Blackstone's *Commentaries on the Laws of England* (1765). Blackstone was the first professional teacher of the common law at the highest level of scholarship in an English university. His course of lectures at Oxford became a four-volume classic exposition of the law of England in a style and according to a system which won the regard of scholars in other disciplines and the gratitude of generations of students and practising lawyers not only in England but perhaps more influentially in the early years of the library-starved American colonies. Of course the common law was neither so flawless nor so stylish as his work presented it. His great gift was that he could make his book about it appear comprehensive while remaining comprehensible, making the law respectable and accessible to the interested non-lawyer, which of course includes the student beginner.

In the two centuries and more that have followed Blackstone, there has not been a comprehensive treatment of the common law to match his work. The increasing volume and scope of the law has produced monographs on most conceivable topics, while books attempting to cover the whole of the law have become primers. There are the great standard practitioners' works like *Chitty on Contracts* and *Clerk and Lindsell on Torts*, daunting to the beginner but often the easiest to understand because they allow the writer room to explain which a beginners' book does not.

There are the outstanding students' textbooks like *Cheshire and Fifoot on Contract* and *Gower on Company Law* which explain the law with a new elegance that it sometimes does not deserve.

Much of legal writing is poor stuff, more so now than ever, but some of it stands high in English scholarly literature. No one has written better than Maitland or Fifoot or Atkin in England, no one better than Cardozo or Brandeis or Holmes in America, or Dixon in Australia and the list could be extended to include other judges of the Common Law family. Much of the best writing is still to be found in the reports. Some judges still pride themselves on their scholarship and style as some scholars do on their judiciousness. The convention is not quite dead that it is for writers to do the work, at the same time pleasing and persuading.

REFERENCES AND FURTHER READING

Holdsworth W.S., *Sources and Literature of English Law* (Clarendon P., 1925).

Maxwell W.H. and Maxwell L.F., *A Legal Bibliography of the British Commonwealth of Nations I: English Law to 1800* (Sweet and Maxwell, 2nd ed., 1955).

Plucknett T.F.T., *Early English Legal Literature* (Cambridge U.P., 1958).

Winfield P.H., *The Chief Sources of English Legal History* (Harvard U.P., 1925).

Appendix: A List of Rulers in England

THIS list contains the names of all those known to have ruled in England to the present day. Until the middle of the tenth century the country now known as England was not united under one ruler and the names listed here are those of the rulers of large parts only of that country. Edward the Elder, son of Alfred the Great (871–99), ruled the whole of England, though he controlled the Danish kingdom of York through Ragnald, who acknowledged his overlordship in 919. The next three kings of the West Saxons ruled the whole of England for only parts of their reigns: Athelstan 927–39, Edmund 939–40 and 944–6, and Edred at various times between 946 and 955.

From the time of the unification of England the dates of the reigns are well settled. Before then many are quite speculative. There are many gaps in historical knowledge and many conflicting statements in the scanty records. No attempt has been made here to enter the controversies about whether the rulers were entitled to be styled king or not. This list is simplified and its purpose is to give the reader as clear a picture of the sequence of English rulers as possible. About the early kings it is inevitably sometimes clearer than it is accurate. The spellings are those best known to historians. Sometimes their choice has been arbitrary.

For a detailed and scholarly treatment of the problems, the best and most readily available book is Powicke F.M. and Fryde E.B., *A Handbook of British Chronology* (Royal Historical Society, 2nd ed., 1961), which should be the first authority consulted for further information, particularly about primary sources.

KINGS OF KENT

Hengist 455–488
Oeric 488–512
Octa 512–?
Eormenric ?–560
Ethelbert 560–616
Eadbald 616–640

Earconbert 640–664
Egbert I 664–673
Hlothere 673–685
Eadric 685–687
Suaebhard 676–692
Oswini 688–690

Wihtred 690–725
Ethelbert II 725–762 (with Eadbert 725–748 and Eardwulf 725–747)

APPENDIX

Sigered, Eanmund
and Heaberht
762–765
Egbert II 765–780

Ealhmund 784
Eadbert 796–798
Cuthred 798–807
Eadwald 798 or 807

Baldred 825

KINGS OF DEIRA

Aelli 559–588
Kings of Bernicia
588–616
Edwin 616–632

Osric 632–633
Oswald 633–641
also of Bernicia
Oswine 644–651

Ethelwald 651–654
afterwards by
Kings of
Bernicia

KINGS OF BERNICIA

Ida 547–559
Between 559 and
592 the sources
disagree; perhaps
Glappa, Adda;

Ethelric,
Theoderic,
Frithuwold,
Hussa
Ethelfrith 592–616

Edwin (king of
Deira) 616–632
Eanfrith 632–633
Oswald 633–641
Oswiu 641–670

KINGS OF NORTHUMBRIA
(The first five are also kings of Bernicia)

Ethelric 588–592
Ethelfrith 592–616
Edwin 616–632
Oswald 633–641
Oswiu 654–670
Egfrith 670–685
Aldfrith 685–704
Eadwulf 704–705
Osred I 705–716
Coenred 716–718
Osric 718–729
Ceolwulf 729–737
Eadbert 737–758

Oswulf 758
Ethelwald Moll
758–765
Alchred 765–774
Ethelred I 774–779
Elfwald I 779–788
Osred II 788–790
Ethelred I again
790–796
Osbald 796
Eardwulf 796–806
Elfwald II 806–808
Eanred 808–840

Ethelred II
840–844
Redwulf 844
Ethelred II
844–848
Osbert 848–862
Aelle 862
Osbert 867
Egbert I 867–873
Ricsige 873–876
Egbert II 876

KINGS OF MERCIA

Penda 632–654	Beonred 757	Wiglaf 827–840
Oswiu of	Offa 757–796	Beorhtwulf
Northumbria	Egfrith 796	840–852
654–657	Coenwulf 796–821	Burgred 852–874
Wulfhere 657–674	Ceolwulf I	Ceolwulf II
Ethelred 674–704	821–823	874–883
Coenred 704–709	Beornwulf	
Ceolred 709–716	823–825	
Ethelbald 716–757	Ludecan 825–827	

KINGS OF THE EAST ANGLES

Redwald 600–606	Aldwulf 664–713	Ethelred and an
Earpwald 616–627	Alfwold 713–749	Ethelbert
Sigeberht (with	Hun, Beonna and	Athelstan 825
Ecgric for part)	Alberht divided	Ethelweard 850
630–637	the kingdom 749	Edmund 855–870
Anna 637–654	Slight evidence	Oswald 870
Aethelhere 654	until 825,	
Ethelwold 654–664	perhaps an	

KINGS OF THE SOUTH SAXONS

Aelle 477	Eadric 685	Osmundus 758
Cissa 514	Nothelm or Nunna	Oswald 772
Aethelwalh	692–725	Oslac 772
674–680	Watt 692	Aldwulf 791
Berhthun and	Aethelstan 714	Aelhwald ?
Andhun 685	Ethelbert 725–750	

KINGS OF THE EAST SAXONS

Saeberht 616	Saeweard	Sigeberht I
Sexred and	616–617	617–653

APPENDIX

Sigeberht II 653–?
Swithelm ?–664
Sighere and Sebbi
  664–683
Sebbi 683–694

Sigeheard and
  Swaefred 694–?
Offa ?–709
Saelred 709–746

Swaefberht (with
  Saelred?) ?–738
Swithred 746–758
Sigeric 758–798
Sigered 799–825

KINGS OF THE WEST SAXONS (WESSEX)

Cerdic 519–534
Cynric 534–560
Ceawlin 560–591
Ceol 591–597
Ceolwulf 597–611
Cynegils 611–643
Cenwalh 643–672
Seaxburh (female)
  672–674
Aescwine 674–676

Centwine 676–685
Caedwalla 685–688
Ine 688–726
Aethelheard
  726–740
Cuthred 740–756
Sigeberht 756–757
Cynewulf 757–786
Beorhtric 786–802
Egbert 802–839

Ethelwulf 839–855
Ethelbald 855–860
Ethelbert 860–865
Ethelred 865–871
Alfred 871–899
Edward the Elder
  899–924
Athelstan 924–939
Edmund 939–946
Edred 946–955

DANISH KINGDOM OF EAST ANGLIA

Guthrum 880–890   Eric 890–902

SCANDINAVIAN KINGDOM OF YORK

Halfdan 875–883
Guthfrith 883–894
Siefred ?
Cnut ?
Ethelwald 899–902
Halfdan and Eowils
  and Ivar
  902–910
Ragnald 919–921
Sihtric Caoch
  921–927

Guthfrith 927
Athelstan of the
  West Saxons
  927–939
Anlaf Guthfrithson
  939–941
Anlaf Sihtricson
  941–943
Ragnald
  Guthfrithson
  943–944

Edmund of the
  West Saxons
  944–946
Edred of the West
  Saxons 946–948
Eric Bloodaxe
  948–954

APPENDIX

KINGS AND QUEENS OF ENGLAND

Three earlier kings ruled the whole of England for parts of their reigns: Athelstan 927–39; Edmund 939–40 and 944–6; Edred at various times between 946 and 955. The rulers whose names follow ruled the whole of England for the whole of their reigns.

Edwy 955–959
Edgar 959–975
Edward the Martyr 975–978
Ethelred the Unready 978–1013
Swegn Forkbeard 1013–1014
Ethelred 1014–1016
Edmund Ironside 1016
Cnut 1016–1035
Harold Harefoot 1035–1040
Harthacnut 1040–1042
Edward the Confessor 1042–1066
Harold Godwinson 1066
William I 1066–1087
William II 1087–1100
Henry I 1100–1135
Stephen 1135–1154
Henry II 1154–1189
Richard I 1189–1199

John 1199–1216
Henry III 1216–1272
Edward I 1272–1307
Edward II 1307–1327
Edward III 1327–1377
Richard II 1377–1399
Henry IV 1399–1413
Henry V 1413–1422
Henry VI 1422–1461
Edward IV 1461–1470
Henry VI 1470–1471
Edward IV 1471–1483
Edward V 1483
Richard III 1483–1485
Henry VII 1485–1509
Henry VIII 1509–1547
Edward VI 1547–1553
Jane 1553

Mary I 1553–1558
Elizabeth I 1558–1603
James I 1603–1625
Charles I 1625–1649
Interregnum 1649–1653
Oliver Cromwell 1653–1658
Richard Cromwell 1658–1659
Interregnum 1659–1660
Charles II 1660–1685 (his regnal years are treated as 1649–1685)
James II 1685–1688
Interregnum 1688–1689
William III 1689–1702 (with Mary II 1689–1694)
Anne 1702–1714
George I 1714–1727
George II 1727–1760

APPENDIX

George III
1760–1820
(regency
1811–1820)
George IV
1820–1830
William IV
1830–1837

Victoria
1837–1901
Edward VII
1901–1910
George V
1910–1936
Edward VIII 1936

George VI
1936–1952
Elizabeth II 1952
to date

Index and Glossary

ABJURE THE REALM. Those who survived the ordeal were required to swear on oath that they would go into exile, which was called abjuring the realm. After the ordeal was abolished, abjuration was still demanded until 1531 of those who took sanctuary in a church to avoid criminal charges, and by Elizabeth I of religious dissidents, 23
Aborigines, Australian, 9
Abridgment, 117, 119
Accidents, 81, 85, 88, 91
Account, 99
Ac etiam, 100, 101
Action, forms of action, 41–50, 65–6, 72–3, 84–96, 99–102
Action on the case, *see* Case
Administration, 18, 19, 25, 31–51, 64–5, 103–4
Admiralty, 104
Ad scaccarium, *see* Exchequer
Adultery, 8
Affidavit, 66
Africa, 1, 9
Agrarian revolution, 52
Agreement, 92–8
Agriculture, agricultural worker, peasant, 32–3, 51–4
Aids, 57–9
Alderman. In Anglo-Saxon times an ealdorman was a high official of noble birth, whom the king put in charge of a shire. In modern times a senior councillor of municipal corporations was called an alderman. Now an honorary title in London and English counties, 13
Alfred (the Great) (871–901), 12, 14, 17
Alienability, alienation, *see* Conveyance
All England Reports, 119
Allodial ownership, 53
Ambush, 21, 26
Amercement. An offender against the king's peace or the peace of a lord was in his mercy (*in misericordia, a merci*), and might have to pay a money penalty called an amercement which was fixed by custom. Magna Carta said that if the amount was not so fixed it must be appropriate to the means of the offender and be assessed by his peers. Amercements were gradually replaced by fines and statutory penalties, 25, 27, 42, 82
America, *see* United States
Ancren Riwle, 112
Andrew II of Hungary, 4
Angles, 11
Anglo-Saxon, 107, 116; *see also* English
Anglo-Saxons, 11–18, 20, 22, 26, 30–1, 41, 82, 92–3
Animals, 88; *see also* Pigs, Horse, Cattle
Appeal. An appeal is now a procedure whereby judgement of a court is reviewed by a higher court but its early meaning in the common law was an accusation of felony, 24, 29, 101–4, 109
Army, *see* Military service
Arrest, 16, 43
Arson. The setting fire to another's dwelling wilfully and maliciously, 24
Assault, 19
Assize, assizes, possessory assizes. An assize first meant a sitting or session, though the word also had the connotation of fixed or established. The term was used for different institutions: legislation, e.g. the Assize of Clarendon; the Grand Assize of Henry II enacted that questions of seisin should be tried by a new procedure which took the name of assize; other procedures were given the name, e.g. the assize of novel disseisin and the assize of *mort d'ancestor*;

Magna Carta provided that these procedures should be held in the shire where the disputed land was and the judges who were sent every year to hear such disputes became known as assize judges and their sessions as assizes, which were abolished only in 1971, 22–3, 25–6, 37, 45–6, 64, 117
Assize of Clarendon (1166), 22–3, 117
Assize of Northampton (1176), 22–3, 117
Assize of Novel Disseisin, 25, 45–6
Assumpsit, 49, 76, 96
Athelstan (924–39), 12–13
Athens, 92
Atkin, Law Lord and legal scholar (1867–1944), influential partly because of his persuasive style, 120, 122
Attorney, *see* Lawyers; *see also* Power of attorney
Audley, Lord Chancellor (1488–1544), Thomas Audley succeeded Thomas More as Lord Chancellor. He was 'ever willing to submit to any degradation and to participate in any crime' on behalf of Henry VIII, 77
Australia, 1, 30, 122

BACON, FRANCIS (1561–1626), Sir Francis Bacon was a lawyer of outstanding intellect, as well as a scientist and philosopher. He became Lord Chancellor under James I in 1618 and succeeded in establishing the ascendancy of equity over common law in matters where their rules conflicted. He was a willing tool of the king but that was not enough to save him from disgrace, a huge fine and a very brief imprisonment when convicted of taking bribes. A much better historian than Coke, 2, 102
Bacon, Matthew (*c.*1690–1760), legal author, 120
Bailiff, 31, 37
Baker, Professor J.H., legal historian, 66, 113, 121
Bankruptcy, 28
Bargain, bargain and sale, 79, 96–7

Baron, *see* Lord
Barons of the Exchequer, 101
Barrister, *see* Lawyers
Base tenures, *see* Tenures
Bastard, *see* Legitimacy
Battle, *see* Trial by battle
Becket, Thomas (1118–70), Archbishop Becket (or à Becket), an English civil lawyer who had studied in Italy, became Chancellor to Henry II in 1154. A worldly priest, he surprisingly became devout when he was made Archbishop of Canterbury, and was eventually murdered in Canterbury Cathedral for opposing the jurisdiction of the royal courts over clergy, 34
Benedeis l'Apostile (12th century), earliest surviving writer in French in England, 106
Beneficiary, beneficial ownership, *see* Cestui que use; *see also* Ownership
Bereford, William (14th century), Chief Justice of the Common Pleas 1309–26, 84
Bible, Gospels, 109–10
Bill, petition, querela, 41, 64–6, 68, 100–3; *see also* Middlesex, Bill of Middlesex
Bishop, 12–14, 17, 28–30, 67, 103
Blackacre. When lawyers talk about a hypothetical piece of land, they call it Blackacre. If there is a second piece, they call it Whiteacre. It is convenient not to be more original
Black Death (1348–50). An epidemic of bubonic plague. The increase in England's population was checked in the early 14th century by famine and reduced by bubonic and pneumonic plague, starting in 1348 and breaking out from time to time until the 17th century, carried by rats and worst in ports and cities, where rats were numerous. Prices fell and wages rose, nearly doubling between 1348 and 1360. The government tried to protect the interest of the rich by fixing wages and restricting movement of labour, leading to the Peasants' Revolt of 1381, 90, 106

INDEX AND GLOSSARY

Blackstone, Sir William (1723–80), first Vinerian Professor of Law at Oxford and later judge of King's Bench and then Common Pleas, author of *Commentaries on the Laws of England*, 113, 121–2
Bond, 94
Bonded maid, 110
Books, law books, 31, 39, 42–44, 74–5, 108, 110–12, 114, 116–22
Borh, 13
Borough, borough courts, 12–14, 32–3, 116
Bot, botleas, bootless, Bot was the compensation paid in Anglo-Saxon times by a wrongdoer to the victim or his or her family to avoid a feud or vengeance. *Botleas* or bootless crimes were those for which punishment could not be bought off, 21, 24, 26
Bracton, Henry de Bracton was probably born in the early years of the 13th century and died in 1268. He was a judge from about 1245. He wrote *De Legibus et Consuetudinibus Angliae*, On the Laws and Customs of England, the first systematic treatment of the whole of English common law, based on decided cases arranged according to Roman Law models. His own manuscript notes are in the British Library, 93–4, 120–1
Brandeis, Louis D. (1856–1941), Associate Justice of the Supreme Court of the United States of America and fine legal writer, 122
Breach, 81, 91, 94
Brevia de cursu, 41, 43, 49
Bribery, 3, 36, 51
British Empire, 104
Britton. Legal textbook in French, written by an unknown author about 1290, 121
Brooke, Robert (died 1558), author of *Abridgement* 1568, 119
Brownlow, R., law reporter, 111
Bullen and Leake, authors of *Precedents of Pleadings*, 120
Burrow, J., law reporter, 113

CALAIS, 109
Cambridge, 102

Canada, 1
Canon law, *see* Ecclesiastical courts
Canons of descent, 60, 70–1
Canterbury Tales, poem in English by Geoffrey Chaucer (1340?–1400), 109
Canute, Cnut (1016–35), 13, 16, 21
Capias, 66
Capital, capitalism, 2, 32, 51–2, 56, 62, 80, 90, 97
Capital punishment, capital offence, *see* Death penalty
Capite, tenant in (pronounced 'kappity'), *see* Tenant in chief
Cardozo, Benjamin N. (1870–1938), Associate Justice of the United States Supreme Court and outstanding legal writer and scholar, 122
Carriage, 87–8
Carrier, 86, 94
Case, action on the case, special case, 48–9, 84–90, 95, 99
Cattle, 16, 81, 92
Celts, 11
Cestui que use (pronounced 'setticky yuce'), beneficiary, 75–80
Champerty, 89
Chancellor, Lord Chancellor, 28, 43, 64–9, 76, 102–3
Chancellor of the Exchequer, The Chancellor of the Exchequer. The name still used in England for the Minister of Finance, must at no time be confused with the Chancellor, or Lord Chancellor who, as well as being the top judge and the Speaker of the House of Lords is also Minister of Justice, 103
Chancery, chancery clerks (*for* Court of Chancery *see* Equity), 40–4, 49, 64–9, 76, 85, 100–4, 105, 119
Channel Islands, 104
Charles I (1625–45), 111
Charles II (1660–85), 111
Charles the Simple, tenth century French king, 105
Charondas, 92
Charter, 108
Chattels, *see* Goods
Chaucer, Geoffrey (1340?–1400), *see* Canterbury Tales
Chelsea Pensioner. A retired serviceman who lives in a hostel in

London and wears a splendid red uniform coat and old-fashioned cap, 28
Cheshire and Fifoot on Contract. Standard students' text on the English law, 122
Chief Justice, Lord Chief Justice, 40, 103
Child, see Infant
China, 11
Chitty on Contracts, standard practitioners' textbook, 122
Chivalry, chivalrous tenures, 53; see also Tenures
Church, 8, 11–12, 15–17, 20, 22–3, 30, 33–5, 51, 64, 70, 106, 116
Church courts, see Ecclesiastical courts
City, 32, 33
Civil law, 19–20, 24, 30, 34; the civil law, 1, 102. 'Civil' is a word which takes its meaning from the word it is contrasted with. Usually in this book it is the criminal law with which civil law is contrasted. In other contexts it could be ecclesiastical or military. Civil law is here used to describe all the law which is not criminal. The civil law, on the other hand, describes the law of most of the countries of western Europe, seen to be derived at least in part from the Roman law of Justinian's *Corpus Juris*, and distinguished from what in English is called the common law
Clarendon, see Assize of Clarendon (1166); see also Constitutions of Clarendon
Class, 2, 9, 26, 66, 68, 87
Clergy, priest, 13–17, 22–3, 64–65, 68, 106
Clerk and Lindsell on Torts, standard practitioners' textbook, 122,
Close, A piece of privately owned land, 83
Code, codification, 11
Coke, Sir Edward (1552–1634). A bullying lawyer who built his fortunes by savagely attacking the political opponents of Elizabeth I and James I, becoming Chief Justice of the Common Pleas in 1606 and of King's Bench in 1613.

He was removed from office in 1616 when he sought to protect the interests of the common lawyers from attacks by the royal prerogative. Profoundly learned in the old law, he wrote about it clearly and convincingly. He has had greater influence on the development of legal rules than any other English lawyer. He is not a reliable historian. He wrote the first textbook on the modern common law, his *Institutes*, and made a collection of reports of important cases, with commentary, which together have always been treated as of very high authority, 2, 102, 110, 118, 121
Collateral relatives, 70–1
Colony, colonialism, 1–2, 9, 19, 31, 35, 37, 116
Combat, see Trial by battle
Commerce, 26, 48, 51, 62, 87, 92–8
Commercial law, 2, 87, 92
Common calling, 86, 95, 98
Common employment, see Fellow servant rule
Common law, 1–4, 17–18, 37–44, 52–7, 64–71, 75–6, 89–91, 93, 98–9, 102–4, 105, 114, 116, 118, 121–2
Common law courts, see King's courts
Common Law Procedure Acts (1852 and 1854), 49, 86
Common Pleas, 25, 38–40, 93–4, 99–102, 104, 118–19, 121
Common recovery, 72–3
Commons, see House of Commons
Commonwealth. The Parliamentary opposition to Charles I executed him in 1649 and abolished the monarchy. From then to the restoration of Charles II in 1660, a period of military government under Oliver Cromwell, Lord Protector, is the period of the Commonwealth, 103, 111
Communal society, communal courts, local courts, 4–18, 21–2, 31–2, 41, 43, 53, 66, 81, 83–4, 92–3, 99–104
Company, limited liability, 51
Compensation, 13-15, 19, 21, 26–7, 43, 81–2, 91

INDEX AND GLOSSARY 133

Comptroller of the Royal Household. One of the king's accountants, 103
Computers, 120
Comyns, Sir John (1667–1740), Chief Baron of the Exchequer, author of the *Digest of the Laws of England*, 120
Conciliar courts, *see* Council
Conquest, *see* Norman Conquest
Conspiracy, 89, 99
Constable, 37
Constitution, constitutional law, 3–4, 116
Constitutions of Clarendon (1164), legislation of Henry II intended to restrict the powers of the ecclesiastical courts, 117
Consumers, 98
Contingent remainder, *see* Remainder
Contract, 7, 14, 16, 35, 47, 49, 51–2, 54, 67, 81–2, 91, 92–98
Contributory negligence, 88
Conveyance, conveyancing, transfer, alienation, alienability, 52, 59–63, 70, 74, 77–80
Convicts, 104
Copyhold, 33
Coram Rege (pronounced 'reejy'), *see* King's Bench
Corpus Juris of Justinian 535, 11
Corruption, *see* Bribery
Council, *see* Curia Regis *and* Privy Council
Council of Law Reporting, 119
Counsel, *see* Lawyers
Count, *see* Narrator
Country, putting oneself on the, 24; *see also* Jury
County, *see* Shire
Court, *see* Common law courts, Common Pleas, Communal courts, Curia Regis, Ecclesiastical courts, Exchequer, King's Bench, King's courts, Leet, Piepowder, Privy Council, Royal courts, Shire, Star Chamber, 19–20, 25–6, 30–44, 52, 62, 64–6, 90, 92, 96–104, 106–7, 112
Covenant, 66, 93, 95, 99
Coventry. To send people to Coventry means to ostracize them, to banish them from the community. The origin of the expression is unknown, though the subject of much speculation, 21
Cranmer, Archbishop Thomas (1489–1556), 110
Crecy, battle of (1346), 109
Credit, 8, 92, 101
Crime, criminal law, 6, 12–15, 19–30, 36–7, 45, 82–3, 89–90, 102–3
Cromwell, Thomas (1485?–1540). The son of a blacksmith, Thomas Cromwell rose to hold the highest offices under Henry VIII, whom he served with ability and zeal. He had seen the excesses of the Pope at first hand and was instrumental in the dissolution of the English monasteries and the Reformation. Henry VIII had him beheaded in 1540. Oliver Cromwell, the Lord Protector at the time of the Commonwealth, was descended from Thomas's sister, 77
Crown, *see* King
Crown, pleas of the, *see* Pleas of the crown
Crusades. The Crusades were holy wars intended to secure Christian control of Jerusalem. The first in which the English were involved was led by Robert, son of William the Conqueror in 1096. Richard I defeated Saladin in the third crusade in 1191. The last was attempted at the end of the 14th century, 39, 75
Curia regis (pronounced 'reejis'), 37–8, 59, 64 102–4; *see also* Privy Council
Current Law, contemporary legal digest and noter-up, 117
Cursitors, 41
Curtesy, 72
Custom, customary law, customary tenure, 2–3, 5–18, 30–32, 38, 41, 54, 57, 66, 83, 93, 97, 102, 104, 116

DAMAGE, loss, damages, 47, 67, 76, 81–2, 85–7, 90, 95, 101
Danelaw, 14
Danes, 11, 13, 20, 22, 105
Death, 55, 57–61, 70–7, 80
Death duties, 80

Death penalty, capital punishment, 15, 21–2, 24–9, 37
Debt, 45, 66, 75, 93–4, 96–102
Deceit, see Fraud
Dedimus potestatem. The Chancery issued this writ to authorize commissioners to examine witnesses out of court on oath, 66
De Donis Conditionalibus, see Statute of Westminster II 1285
Deed, 66, 79, 93–4
De ejectione firmae, 47
Defamation, 89–90
Defences, 27–8
Delay, 12, 68
Demesne, 33
Detinue, 42, 45, 93, 99
Dialect, 105
Dictatorship, see Tyranny
Digest, *The Digest*, 119–20
Disseisin, see seisin; see also Assize of novel disseisin
Divine service, 53, 56; see also Tenures
Dixon, Sir Owen (1886–1972), Chief Justice of the High Court of Australia, and legal stylist, 122
Doctor and Student, Christopher St Germain wrote two dialogues in 1523 called *Dialogue on the Foundations of the Law and on Conscience*, and known since as *Doctor and Student*. The doctor of the title is an ecclesiastical lawyer, seeking to understand the common law by questioning the expert, called the student of the laws of England. In learning about the common law, the doctor subjects it to the tests of conscience and canon law ideas, 75, 110, 121
Doe, John, a fictitious litigant, 48
Domesday Book. A survey of the manors of England, begun in 1085, by commissioners sent by William the Conqueror to ask the extent of the manor, who owned it then and who in the time of Edward the Confessor, its value at those times, and the kind of tenure, so that he might have a full account of all his conquered lands, 31, 74
Donoghue v. *Stevenson* [1932] A.C. 562. A leading case in the law of torts, in which the judgment of Lord Atkin laid down the vague principle upon which the modern action of negligence has since been based. It arose from an action for damages for injury suffered from drinking ginger beer from an opaque bottle in which were the decomposed remains of a snail, 86, 91
Dower, 35, 72
Duty of care, see Negligence
Dyer, Sir James (1512–82), Chief Justice of Common Pleas and author of the first modern reports, 110, 118

EADRIC (685–7), 15
Ealdorman, 12; see also Alderman
Earl of Oxford's Case [1615] 1 Chancery Reports 1, 67, 69, 102
Ecclesiastical courts, church courts, canon law, 30, 34–5, 64, 70, 90, 93, 103–4, 109, 116
Economics, economy, 2–11, 54–63, 90–1, 97–8
Edgar (959–75), 13
Education, legal, 102, 106, 112, 114, 118–21
Edward the Confessor (1042–66), 105
Edward I (1272–1307), 21
Edward II (1307–27), 47
Edward III (1327–77), 41
Edward IV (1461–83), 103
Ejectment, 44, 46–8, 76, 99
Eldon, Lord (1751–1838). Unusually conservative, even for a high-ranking judge, he became Lord Chancellor in 1801 and kept the office except for one year until 1821, successfully stifling much needed reform through his influence in the government. He had the most subtle legal mind of his time and a complete command of the common law and equity. His inability to make up his mind led to long delays and the denial of justice in the court of Chancery, 68
Elizabeth I (1558–1603), 103
Ellenborough, Lord (1750–1818), Chief Justice of King's Bench 1802–18. Like his contemporary Eldon he was implacable in his

INDEX AND GLOSSARY

opposition to reform and successful through his political influence. His arrogant anti-humanitarian zeal was even more destructive than Eldon's, leading to the continuance of cruelty and oppression in the criminal law long after the need for reform had been shown, 29

Ellesmere, Lord (1540?–1617). Chancellor from 1603, he did much to establish the ascendancy of equity over the common law, 67

Employment, employer, worker, master, servant, 85–91; *see also* Slavery

Encyclopedia of Forms and Precedents. Standard handbook of practitioners, providing precedents for non-litigious purposes, 120

England, English, Old English, 105–7, 110, 117, 122

English and Empire Digest, 120

English Reports, 119

Englishry, presentment of, *see* Presentment of Englishry

Enrolment, *see* Register

Entail, *see* Fee tail

Entries, books of, 120

Entry, forcible entry, 21

Equity, courts of equity, Court of Chancery, 2, 35, 64–9, 75–80, 94, 99–104

Escheat, 57–9

Estates, 53–4, 60–3, 71–80

Ethelbert I (560–616), 11, 13–15

Ethelred (978–1013, 1014–16), 105

Europe, 34

Evidence, 22–3, 42–3, 66, 84, 92–4, 96, 107–10

Exchange, 92, 97

Exchequer, Court of Exchequer, Exchequer of Pleas, 35, 38–40, 99–102, 108, 119

Execution, in the sense of formally signing a document, 77; in relation to the Statute of Uses, 78; in the sense of judicial killing *see* Death penalty

Exile, 23

Eyre, justices in eyre, articles of the eyre, 23–5, 36–7, 41, 64, 108, 118

FACTORY, 82, 87, 110

Fair, *see* Market

Family, kin 6–9, 12–17, 27, 62, 70–6, 82

Fealty, 13, 55; *see also* Homage

Fee simple, 61–3, 72–4, 76, 78–9

Fee tail, entail, estate tail, 62, 71–4, 79–80

Fellow servant rule, 88

Felony, appeal of felony 23–4, 27, 37, 59, 83, 89–90

Feoffee to uses, feoffment, feoffor (pronounced 'feffee, feffment, feffor'), 75–8

Feud, 8, 13–14, 20, 26, 45, 81–3; *see also* Tribal fighting

Feudal court, *see* Seignorial court

Feudal system, 13, 31–40, 52-63, 73–4

Fictions, 42–48, 52, 72–7, 84, 95, 99–101

Fifoot, C.H.S. (1899–1975). Legal historian and master of English prose style, 84, 91

Fiji, 1

Fine, as a monetary penalty for crime, 25, 27, 42, 64, 67, 82; as a money payment from a feudal tenant to his lord, 59–60

Fitzherbert, Sir Anthony (1470–1538), Justice of Common Pleas and scholarly legal author, 119

Fitznigel, Richard (died 1198), justice and treasurer, author of *Dialogus de Scaccario*, 108

Fleet prison, 66

Folk-moot, 13–14

Forfeiture, 21, 24, 28, 37, 58-9

Formalities, 92

Formedon, 62, 73

Forms, formula, 41, 84, 87, *for* Forms of action *see* Action

Fortescue, Sir John (1394?–1476?), Chief Justice of King's Bench, 110

France, *see* French

Franchise, 31, 33, 66, 116

Franciscans, 75

Frankalmoign, 53, 56; *see also* Tenures

Fraud, 67, 75, 77, 94–5

Freedom of contract, 97–8

Freehold, 46, 89

Free tenures, *see* Tenures

French, France, 105–15, 117

Future interests, 73–4

INDEX AND GLOSSARY

GAOL DELIVERY, 25
Gipsies, 28
Glanvill, Ranulph de Glanvill became Chief Justiciar of England in 1180. He was also a soldier and statesman of Henry II. He died in Acre on a Crusade with Richard I in 1190. His name is given to the earliest textbook of the common law, his *Tractatus de Legibus et Consuetudinibus Angliae*, Treatise on the Laws and Customs of England. It was probably written by (dictated to?) his secretary, Hubert Walter about 1188, 39, 120
Golden Bull 1222. A compact between Andrew II, king of Hungary, and his nobles, setting limits to royal authority, 4
Goods, chattels, 28, 42, 45–6, 83, 92–4, 97
Gospels, *see* Bible
Gower, John (1325?–1408), trilingual English (or Welsh) poet, 106
Gower, L.C.B., legal scholar, author of *Modern Company Law*, 122
Grammar, 114
Gramophone, 108
Grand jury, *see* Jury
Grant, grantor, 36, 70–9, 92
Guardian, 58

HABEAS CORPUS. A writ which commands a person alleged to be unjustly detaining another to bring that person before the court. It has sometimes been effective to prevent a person being deprived of freedom illegally, though there are countless examples of its inefficacy against royal tyrants. The Latin *Habeas corpus* means: 'you should have the body'. (Pronounced 'hay-be-ass'), 3
Hale, Sir Matthew (1609–76), Justice of Common Pleas, Baron of the Exchequer and Chief Justice of King's Bench, legal scholar and prolific writer, 121
Halsbury's Laws of England. The major encyclopedia of English law, named after its first general editor, Lord Halsbury (1823–1921), Lord Chancellor, 120

Halsbury's Statutes. A standard set of annotated statutes, 117
Hanging, *see* Death penalty
Harding, Alan, legal historian, 26, 40
Harold (Godwinson) (1066), 20, 35, 105
Harold Hardrada, king of the Danes, 20
Hazeltine H.D., legal historian, 16
Heaven v. Pender [1883] 11 Q.B.D. 503, 86, 91
Heir, heritability, inheritance, succession, 30, 34, 46, 55–62, 70–80
Henry I (1100–35), 106
Henry II (1154–89), 22, 34, 36, 39, 106
Henry III (1216–72), 24, 39
Henry VII (1485–1509), 103, 114
Henry VIII (1509–47), 67, 77–8, 102, 114
Hide. The hide in Anglo-Saxon and Norman times was a measurement of land but not of uniform area. It at first seems to have been quantified according to its productivity. Though surprising to modern minds, land in communal societies is sometimes measured not according to its boundaries but in other ways more appropriate in the eyes of the inhabitants, 14
High Court of Judicature, 104
Hlothere (673–85), 15
Holdsworth, Sir William S. (1871–1944). Vinerian Professor of English Law at Oxford, author of the comprehensive *History of English Law*, 114
Holmes, Oliver Wendell (1841–1935), Associate Justice of the United States Supreme Court (1902–32) and great scholar of the law, its history and theory. He wrote *The Common Law* (1881), a history which is full of insights and originality, *vii*, 122
Homage. A man who took a grant of land did homage to the grantor, thereby making himself the grantor's man ('*home*' in Norman French). He would then also swear fealty to his new lord. Homage and

INDEX AND GLOSSARY

fealty were the basic bonds of feudalism, 55–60
Homicide, *see* Murder
Hong Kong, 90, 108, 110
Horse, 95
House of Commons, 26, 76
Hue and cry, 14
Hundred, hundred court, 14, 22, 30–4
Hungary, 4

IMPRISONMENT, prison, 25, 43, 64, 66–7, 76, 84, 100, 103, 112
In Banco, see Common Pleas
Incidents, 55–60, 75–9
Income, 55, 57, 60, 62
In Consimili Casu, 49, 85
Indebitatus assumpsit, see Assumpsit
India, 1
Indictment, 23–6, 37
Individual, 6–9, 11, 13, 20, 22, 53, 80, 90, 98
Indo-European language, 112
Industrial relations, 26
Industrial revolution, 26, 48, 51, 85
Ine (688–726), 11, 16
Infant, child, minor, 55–9, 110
Inflation, 59, 83
Information. Information is the name given to different kinds of procedures but most commonly to the first step in a criminal prosecution to enforce a penalty or before magistrates, 26
Informers, 26
Inheritance, *see* Heir
Innkeepers, 86, 94
Inns of court. From the 14th century there have been in London hostels which accommodated lawyers and students of law. The four great Inns of Court are the last ones to remain. They are Gray's Inn, Inner Temple, Middle Temple and Lincoln's Inn. They are responsible for the education and professional conduct of barristers in England, and have many privileges, 102
Inquest, 22, 27, 37
Inrollments of Acts of Parliament, 117
Institutes of the Laws of England, 121, *see also* Coke
Insurance, 91
International law, 5–6

Inter vivos. This term is used to distinguish a transaction intended to take effect during the life of the parties from a will, which takes effect on the death of the testator, 72
Intestacy, 71
Ireland, Irish, 112
Islam, 30
Issue, 62, 70–4

JAMES I (1602–25), 2, 102
Japan, 1, 11
Jessel, Sir George (1824–83), Master of the Rolls, 97
Jews, 34
John (1199–1216), 24, 39
Judges, 2–3, 19, 24–9, 35–40, 41, 44, 64, 67–8, 85–7, 95–7, 100–4, 111–12, 116, 118–19, 121
Judgment, 110
Judicature Acts (1871–3), 49, 68, 104
Jurisdiction, 24, 30–43, 64–8, 83, 94, 99–104, 115
Jury, grand jury, petty jury, 18, 22–8, 43–5, 66, 85, 96, 112
Justice, 3, 11, 15, 22, 24, 37, 42, 64–8, 87, 95, 98, 111–12
Justices, *see* Judges
Justices of the peace, 25–6
Justiciars, 35–9
Justinian (483–565), 11
Jutes, 11

KENT, 11, 15
Kin, *see* Family
King, Crown, 11–18, 22–9, 30–40, 41–5, 49, 52–60, 64–5, 76–8, 82–3, 101–8, 110, 117
King's Bench, 25, 38–40, 42, 96, 99–104, 118–20
King's courts, common law courts, 33–44, 52, 54, 56, 64–8, 70, 83–4, 90, 93–7, 99–104
King's peace, *see* Peace
Knight, knight service, 32, 52–3, 56–9, 78

LABOUR, 2, 87, 90, 97
Laissez-faire, 7, 97
Land, 7, 25, 28, 31–3, 37, 41, 44–8, 52–63, 70–80, 82–4, 88–9, 97, 102
Landlords, landowners, 2, 20, 26,

32–6, 53, 55, 60, 66, 68, 70–80, 106; *see also* Class, Lord
Langland, William (1332?–1400?), author of *The Vision of William Concerning Piers Ploughman*, poem in Middle English, 109
Language, 105–15
Larceny, grand larceny, 24–5, 28
Lateran Council (1215), 23–4
Latin, 105–8, 110–11, 113, 117, 120
Latitat, 100–1
Law, nature of, 3
Law books, *see* Books
Law French, 106–7, 109
Law reform, *see* Reform
Law reports, *see* Reports
Law Reports, The, 119
Lawyers, 2–3, 32, 37, 40, 42, 47, 52, 59, 64, 68–71, 73, 77–80, 86–7, 99, 101–2, 106–15, 118, 120, 122
Lay tenures, *see* Tenures
Lease, leasehold, lease and release, 46–8, 75, 78–80
Leet, court leet, 20
Legal education, *see* Education
Legislation, *see* Statute
Legitimacy, 34, 71, 105
Lessor, lessee, *see* Lease
Libel, 89–90
Liberalism, 97
Liege. A man bound by allegiance to his lord, 14
Life estate, life interest, life tenancy, 54, 60–2, 73–4, 79–80
Limitation, words of, 61
Lineal descendants, 70
Littleton, Sir Thomas (1402–81), Justice of Common Pleas and author of *Tenures*, probably the earliest law book to be printed in England, about 1481, 121
Loan, 94
Local court, *see* Communal court
Local government, 26, 31
Long Parliament, 104
Lord, lord of the manor, baron, 12–14, 16, 28, 30–3, 42–4, 50–62
Lord Chief Justice, *see* Chief Justice
Lord Dacre of the South's Case (1976) 93 Selden Society 228, 77, 80
Lord-Lieutenant, 26
Lord's court, *see* Seignorial courts
Loss, *see* Damage

MAGNA CARTA 1215, 4, 37, 39–40, 58–9, 114
Magnates. The greatest of the nobles, 34
Maiming, 24, 28, 37
Maine, Sir Henry S. (1882–88), legal historian and anthropologist, 7
Maintenance, 89, 99
Maitland, Frederic W. (1850–1906). The outstanding legal historian of the nineteenth and early twentieth centuries, 48, 50, 105, 109–13, 122
Malfeasance, 95
Malice aforethought, 27; *see also* Prosecution, malicious prosecution
Manchester, 20
Manor, manorial system, manorial court, 10, 30, 33, 99, 116
Mansfield, Lord (1705–93), Chief Justice of the King's Bench 1759–1788, he had great influence on the development of the common law, particularly through the incorporation of mercantile custom, which helped to make the law appropriate for the needs of the bourgeoisie, 2–3
Manslaughter, 27
Manuscript, 118
Market, fair, fair courts, 15, 30, 34, 92–3, 97, 116
Marriage, 30, 34, 57–9, 70–1, 79–80, 108
Mary I (1553–8), 67
Mary Portington's Case [1613] 10 Coke's Reports 35, 73, 80
Master, *see* Employment
Master of the Rolls, The Lord Chancellor's assistant and keeper of records, he is now the president of the Court of Appeal, 68
Maud, queen of Henry I (1080–1118), 106
Merchants, 34, 68, 93
Micronesia, 2
Middle class, *see* Class
Middlesex, Bill of Middlesex, 42, 100
Military dictatorship, *see* Tyranny
Military service, military power, army, 22, 52–60, 78, 111
Milsom, S.F.C., legal historian, 29, 61, 65
Mine, 110

INDEX AND GLOSSARY

Minor, *see* Infant
Misdemeanour, 23, 83, 90
Misfeasance, 86
Moneylenders, 98
Monopolies, 63
Moore, Serjeant. A 16th century serjeant of the Common Pleas, 79
Moots, 113
More, Sir Thomas (1477–1535), Chancellor to Henry VIII, scholar and friend of Erasmus, beheaded for opposing the king's attempts to change his successors, and his claim to be head of the church of England. Author of *Utopia*, 67, 77
Mort d'ancestor, 61
Mosley, Sir Oswald, ancestor of the fascist, 20
Motor car, 91, 95
Murder, homicide, *murdrum*, 19, 22, 24–7

NARRATOR, narration, counter, count, 109, 112, 120
Natura Brevium, 121
Negligence, 85–8, 95
New Tenures, 121
New Zealand, 1, 91
Next of kin, 46
Nisi Prius (pronounced 'nigh-sigh pry-us'), 25
Nonfeasance, 86, 95
Norman, Norman Conquest (1066), 10, 12, 17–23, 27, 30–6, 41, 51–6, 60, 64, 82–3, 105–8, 113, 116
Normandy, 22, 27, 31–2, 37
Norsemen, 12
North, Sir Francis (1637–85), Chief Justice of Common Pleas, uncle of Roger North, who wrote about him in *Lives of the Norths* (1735), 112
Northampton, Assize of, *see* Assize of Northampton (1176)
Nottingham, Lord (1621–82), Lord Chancellor 1675–82, he developed the principles of equity, particularly trusts, which to some extent made up for his part in the drafting of the Statute of Frauds 1677, 68
Novae Narrationes, 120
Nova Statuta, 117
Novel disseisin, *see* Assize of Novel Disseisin
Nuisance, 89

OATH, oath-helpers, 14, 17, 22–3, 43, 55, 66, 76, 94
Occupiers' liability, 89
Old English, *see* English
Old Tenures, 121
Ordeal, 22–4, 67
Ordinance, 22; *see also* Statute
Outlaw, 12, 21
Ownership, 52–3, 60–1, 72–5
Oxford, 102, 112, 117, 121; *see also* Provisions of Oxford
Oyer and terminer, 43, 64

PACIFIC, 1
Pakistan, 1
Papua New Guinea, 1, 9, 104, 108
Pardon, 27
Paris, 113
Parliament, 2, 43, 69, 73, 97, 102–4, 109–11, 116–17
Parol contracts, contracts not made by deed, even if written, 94
Particular estate, 73–4
Peace, king's peace, law and order 13–6, 18–33, 39, 45–6, 49–51, 55, 66, 82–3, 90, 95, 103, 112
Peasant, *see* Agricultural worker
Peasants' Revolt (1381). Popular uprisings against widespread oppression, particularly the Poll Tax. The leader, Wat Tyler, was treacherously killed at a parley with the king, Richard II, who did not keep the promises extracted from him to free the villeins, 90
Performance, 95–8
Personal action, personalty, personal property, 46, 99
Peterborough Chronicle, 112
Petition, *see* Bill
Petty sessions, 26
Philippines, 2
Piepowder (pronounced 'pie powder'), Courts of. The name given to courts held at certain fairs in the Middle Ages. The derivation is unknown, 34
Piers Ploughman, *see* Langland
Pigs, 81–2
Pin Money. An allowance made to a wife for personal expenses, 79
Plague, *see* Black Death, 84, 106
Plantations, 104; *see also* Colony

Plato (c.428–348BC), Greek philosopher, 92
Plea, Pleas of the Crown, 21, 27, 39, 109
Pleading, 109–11, 118, 120
Plea roll, 120
Plowden, Edmund (1518–85), legal scholar and early reporter, 110, 118
Poaching, 26
Poitiers, battle of (1356), 109
Police, 10, 13, 26, 29, 54
Policy, politics, 73, 81–2, 86–91, 96–9, 102
Posse Comitatus. Latin for 'the power of the county', the name of the band of men summoned by the sheriff to enforce a writ or defend the county from the king's enemies, 13
Possession, 45–7, 73, 75–6, 89
Possessory assizes, see Assize
Potter, Harold, legal historian, 21
Power, 51–2, 68, 70, 81, 97
Power of attorney, 75
Praecipe (pronounced 'pressipy'), 44
Praecipe Quod Recipiat Homagium, 60
Precedents. (In England pronounced 'pressidents', elsewhere often 'preecidents'), 42, 120
Presentment of Englishry, 20, 27
Priest, see Clergy
Primer seisin, 57–9
Primitive law, primitive society, see Customary Law, Communal society
Printing, 90, 118, 120
Printing and Numerical Registering Co. v. Sampson [1875] 19 L.R. Equity 462, 97
Prison, see Imprisonment
Privilege, 111–12
Privy Council, 26, 103–4; see also Curia Regis
Procedure, 18, 22–4, 29–31, 34, 36–7, 42–3, 46, 64, 66–7, 69, 76, 85, 99–104
Promise, 92–98
Pronunciation, 113
Proof, see Evidence
Property, 20, 32–5, 43, 50, 52, 55, 57, 59, 61–2, 66, 68, 70, 73, 76, 78, 81, 87
Prosecution, malicious prosecution, 26, 89–90

Protection, 32
Provisions of Oxford (1258), 43, 117
Provocation, 27
Public General Statutes, 117
Public policy, see Policy
Publishers, 119
Punishment, 5, 12, 15, 19–29
Purchase, words of, 61

QUARE EJECIT INFRA TERMINUM, 47
Quarter Sessions, 26
Querela, see Bill
Quia Emptores (1290), 59, 61
Quid pro quo. Something given in return, 95
Quominus, 101

RAILWAYS, 85, 87
Ransom, 57–8
Rape, 24, 28
Rastell, William (1508?–65), legal author and printer, judge of Queen's Bench, 117, 120
Raymond, Lord (1673–1733), Chief Justice of King's Bench, 111
Real action, realty, real property, 46–8, 72–3, 76, 89, 99, 121
Record, 106–7, 113–14
Record Commission, 117
Reeve, 11, 13, 31
Reform, law reform, 29, 52, 73, 97, 106–7
Regenbald, (eleventh century), probably first Chancellor (of Edward the Confessor) about 1065, 105
Register, registration, 78–9
Registrum Omnium Brevium, 120
Relief, 57, 59
Religion, religious landholding, 7–8, 10, 33, 54, 75
Remainder, remainderman, 73–4, 76, 79–80
Remedy, 81, 93, see also Damages
Rent, 112
Rentcharge, 79
Reports, law reports, reporters, 2, 110, 116, 118–9, see also Year Books
Restoration, 114
Resulting use, 77
Retaliation, see Feud
Returna Brevium, 120
Revenue, see Tax and income
Reversion, reversioner, 73–4, 79

INDEX AND GLOSSARY 141

Richard I (1189–99), 39
Risk, 81, 88, 91, 97
Roads, 85
Robbery 112; *see also* Theft
Roe, Richard, 48
Rollo, Duke of Normandy (tenth century), 105
Roman-Dutch law , 1
Roman law, 10, 12, 34, 102
Rome, 10, 12
Royal Courts, *see* King's Courts
Ruffhead, Owen (1723–69), barrister, author, publisher and propagandist, compiled *The Statutes at Large from Magna Charta to 1763* (1762–5), 117
Rylands v. *Fletcher* [1867] L.R. 3 H.L. 330, 88, 91

ST GERMAIN, CHRISTOPHER, *see* Doctor and Student
Sales, 7, 15, 54, 56, 61–2, 77–8, 90, 92
Sanctions, *see* Punishment
Saudi Arabia, 37
Saxons, *see* Anglo-Saxons
School, schoolboy, *see* Education
Scotland, Scots, 111
Scrutton, Lord Justice. Outstanding commercial judge and author of standard text on charterparties, 87
Scutage, 76
Seal, 28, 42, 64, 66, 95
Security, surety, 12, 14, 17
Seignorial rights, seignorial courts, 14, 33
Seisin (pronounced 'seezin'), disseisin. Possession of a freehold estate, exclusive of others; specially protected in medieval law, 45–6, 60, 75–6
Selden Society, 80
Self-help, 20, 23, 45, 82-3
Serf, *see* Slavery
Serjeants-at-Law, 40, 79, 99, 111
Serjeanty, 53, 56; *see also* Tenures
Servant, *see* Employment
Services, 12, 53–60, 75
Settlements, 70–80
Sheriff, 17, 22, 31, 35, 37, 41–4, 83, 100
Shire, county, shire court, county court, 13, 22, 25–6, 30–34, 42, 66, 100, 114, 116

Shropshire, 27
Sicily, 92
Slade's Case [1602] 4 Coke's Rep. 91a, 96, 98
Slander, 90
Slavery, slave, serf, unfree tenure, 2, 14–5, 52, 54, 90; *see also* Villein, Bonded maid
Smith, 95
Smith, Adam, economist, 97
Socage, 53–4, 56–8, 78; *see also* Tenures
Socialism, 7
Solzhenytsyn, Alexander, Russian novelist now in exile, 21
Specialty contract, *see* Deed
Sri Lanka, 1
Star Chamber, Court of, 90, 103–4
State, 2, 6–7, 10, 12, 38, 91, 97–8, 103
Statham, Nicholas (fifteenth century). Author of earliest abridgment (*c*.1490) and Baron of Exchequer, 119
Status, 6–7, 55, 57, 59–61, 86
Statute, 14–5, 24–6, 28, 37, 61, 68–9, 73, 77–8, 89–90, 94, 99–101, 106, 109–10, 114–8; *see also Nova Statuta* and *Vetera Statuta*
Statute of Enrolments (1535), 79
Statute of Gloucester (1278), 24
Statute of Labourers (1349), 90
Statute of Pleading (1362), 109
Statute of Treasons (1350), 28
Statute of Uses (1535), 78–80
Statute of Westminster II (1285), 25, 49, 62, 72–3, 85
Statute of Wills (1540), 78
Statutory torts, 89, 99
Stratford-atte-Bowe. Chaucer mocked the English French of one of his characters by saying that it was the French of Stratford-atte-Bowe, or learned in London, 113
Strict liability, 89
Strip System. From the Norman Conquest to the end of the 14th century, most arable land in England was cultivated in great open fields often many acres in extent and ploughed by heavy ploughs drawn by eight oxen, which divided the field into strips. A peasant would be more likely to

own separated than adjacent strips. Corporate ownership of the ploughteam and corporate efforts were necessary, 32
Stubbs, William (1825–1901), bishop and historian, 106
Student, *see* Education
Subinfeudation, 55, 56, 59, 61; *see also Quia Emptores*
Subpoena, 64, 66
Succession, *see* Heir
Suicide, 24
Surety, *see* Security
Surgeon, 86
Syntax, 113

TAINE, HIPPOLYTE A. (1828–93), French historian, philosopher and critic, 113
Tasmania, 5, 90
Tax, 28, 35, 37–8, 52, 80, 95, 101–2, 106
Technology, 4, 6, 9, 21–3, 43, 46, 48, 85–6, 90, 94
Templars, 109
Tenant, tenant in chief, mesne tenant, 32–3, 44, 53–62, 72–4, 78
Tenures, 53–59
Testator, *see* Will
Testimony, *see* Evidence
Thief, theft, 13–5, 22, 28–9, 93
Thorogood v. *Bryant* [1849] 8 C.B. 115. The case of the injured passenger, (mentioned but not named), 88, 91
Tithing, 13
Title, 47–8, 78; *see also* Ownership; in the sense of honour, 70
Torts, 20, 25, 48–9, 81–91, 95
Torture, 29, 57–8
Trade, 26, 48, 94
Trade union, 87–8, 90
Transfer of land, *see* Conveyance
Treason, high treason, petty treason, 24–5, 28, 58, 89, 103
Treasurer, Treasury, 28, 38, 103, 108
Trespass, 24, 39, 46–9, 76, 81–92, 95–6, 98–100
Trial, 22–6, 37, 103
Trial by battle. Introduced by the Normans, it was (like the ordeal) a reference to divine adjudication. Until Henry II a denial of a claim to own land led to trial by battle, the defendant swearing that the claimant was perjured. Battle was available to a defendant to real actions and the writ of debt. Champions were allowed to take the place of women, infants, men over 60 and those who could acquire the privilege, priests, powerful lords and rich merchants, though not in appeals of felony. The combat took place formally before the judges. Each party had a staff and a shield. They fought until one was defeated. If the defendant held out until dusk, he won. The Lateran Council 1215 condemned battle as well as ordeals but it was only formally abolished in 1819, 23, 45, 67
Tribal fighting, 11, 20, 26, 82; *see also* Feud
Trust, trustees, 67–9, 77, 79–80
Tyranny, dictatorship, military dictatorship, 28, 31-2, 35, 103

UNITED KINGDOM, 117, 119
United States of America, 1, 22, 119, 121
Universities, 102, 107, 121
Urbanization, 5
Uses, 74–80; *see also* Statute of Uses
Usury, 58

VESTING, 74, 80
Vetera Statuta, 117
Veterinarian, 86, 95
Vice-Chancellor. A judge who assisted the Chancellor in the Court of Chancery; now the senior Chancery judge, 68
Villein, villein tenure, villenage, 53, 56; *see also* Tenures, Peasants' Revolt
Viva Voce (pronounced 'vie-va vochy'), by oral examination, 66
Voyage of St Brendan, 106

WAGER OF LAW, 43, 95, 97
Wages, 7
Wales, Welsh, 111
Wapentake (pronounced 'woppen-take'). Danish name for the hundred, 13, 31
War, 5, 7–8, 28

INDEX AND GLOSSARY

Wardship, 57-9, 75
Warranty, 72
Waste, 58
Wealth, 51, 68, 71, 80, 87
Weekly Law Reports, 119
Welfare State, 2, 61
Wer, 21
Wergild, 14
Wessex, 10-11, 13
West Indies, 1
Westminster, Westminster Hall, 25, 39, 41-2, 100
Wig, 107
Wihtred, (690-725), 16
Will, 16-17, 34, 52, 61, 70, 71, 75-8, 93
William I (the Conqueror) (1066-87), 19, 21, 27, 31-2, 34-5, 54, 103, 105-6
William II (1087-1100), 106
Winfield, Sir Percy H. (1878-1958), Cambridge professor and legal author, 116
Winkin de Worde (died about 1534), printer, 120
Witches, 8
Wite, 21, 82
Witnesses, 15-16, 22, 108-9

Wolsey, Cardinal, Henry VIII's Chancellor 1515-30. Developed the Star Chamber. Fell foul of the king and was imprisoned but died before he could be killed, 68
Women, 55-6, 62, 70-1, 79-81. (I hope I have avoided using masculine pronouns to include women. Where they are used intentionally it is because of the unpleasant fact that women were allowed to play only minor roles in the law and its development until modern times)
Worker, *see* Employment
Wounding, 24
Writ, 18, 36, 40-50, 60, 64-5, 76, 83-5, 89, 93-5, 99-101, 106, 108, 117, 120-1
Writ of Right, 23, 44-6
Writing, 93, 107
Wyclif, John (died 1384). Part-author and editor of the first complete translation of the Bible into English, 109

YEAR BOOKS, 40, 108-10, 114, 118-19